NANA'S BOOKS™

Engagement + Nostalgia = Joy™

ROTKEHLCHEN · *Erithacus rubecula* (L.)

HOPE IS THE THING WITH FEATHERS

Hope is the thing with feathers
That perches in the soul
And sings the tune without the words
And never stops - at all
And sweetest, in the Gale, is heard
And sore must be the storm
That could abash the little Bird
That kept so many warm
I ve heard it in the chillest land
And on the strangest Sea
Yet, never, in Extremity,
It asked a crumb of me.

Emily Dickinson

THE REDWING

I hear you, Brother, I hear you,
Down in the alder swamp,
Springing your woodland whistle
To herald the April pomp!
First of the moving vanguard,
In front of the spring you come,
Where flooded waters sparkle
And streams in the twilight hum.
You sound the note of the chorus
By meadow and woodland pond,
Till, one after one up-piping,
A myriad throats respond.

I see you, Brother, I see you,
With scarlet under your wing,
Flash through the ruddy maples,
Leading the pageant of spring.
Earth has put off her raiment
Wintry and worn and old,
For the robe of a fair young sibyl,
Dancing in green and gold.
I heed you, Brother.
To-morrow I, too, in the great employ,
Will shed my old coat of sorrow
For a brand-new garment of joy.

Bliss Carman

HUMMING BIRDS

The Sun Gem and the Brilliant

THE HOMESTEAD

The years, like humming birds,
Just poised a moment on the wing,
To sip the nectar from the cup
Of life's sweet offering;
The homestead's old familiar halls,
The grassy meadow where I played,
The orchard with its melting fruit,
And soft refreshing shade;
The blacksmith-shop where, all day long,
My noble father toiled and sang,
Where in the morning and at eve,
The music of the anvil rang;
The garden with its spreading vines,
Its roses and its daffodils;
The dark old forest in the east;
Beyond the heaven-aspiring hills.

M.P.A. Crozier

NAT. SIZE.

2/5

THE ROBIN

ROBIN REDBREAST

Good-by, good-by to Summer!
For Summer's nearly done;
The garden smiling faintly,
Cool breezes in the sun;
Our thrushes now are silent,
Our swallows flown away,—
But Robin's here in coat of brown,
And scarlet brestknot gay.
Robin, Robin Redbreast,
O Robin dear!
Robin sings so sweetly
In the falling of the year.

Bright yellow, red, and orange,
The leaves come down in hosts;
The trees are Indian princes,
But soon they'll turn to ghosts;
The leathery pears and apples
Hang russet on the bough;
It's autumn, autumn, autumn late,
'T will soon be winter now.
Robin, Robin Redbreast,
O Robin dear!
And what will this poor Robin do?
For pinching days are near.

The fireside for the cricket,
The wheat stack for the mouse,
When trembling night winds whistle
And moan all round the house.
The frosty ways like iron,
The branches plumed with snow,—
Alas! in winter dead and dark,
Where can poor Robin go?
Robin, Robin Redbreast, O Robin dear!
And a crumb of bread for Robin,
His little heart to cheer.

William Allingham

THE MUSIC LESSON

A thrush alit on a young-leaved spray,
And, lightly clinging,
It rocked in its singing
As the rapturous notes rose loud and gay;
And with liquid shakes,
And trills and breaks,
Rippled through blossoming boughs of May.
Like a ball of fluff, with a warm brown throat
And throbbing bosom,
'Mid the apple-blossom,
The new-fledged nestling sat learning by rote
To echo the song
So tender and strong,
As it feebly put in its frail little note.
O blissfullest lesson amid the green grove!
The low wind crispeth
The leaves, where lispeth
The shy little bird with its parent above;
Two voices that mingle
And make but a single
Hymn of rejoicing in praise of their love

Mathilde Blind

THE FIRST BLUEBIRDS

The poor earth was so winter-marred,
Harried by storm so long,
It seemed no spring could mend her,
No tardy sunshine render
Atonement for such wrong.
Snow after snow, and gale and hail,
Gaunt trees encased in icy mail,
The glittering drifts so hard
They took no trace
Of scared, wild feet,
No print of fox and hare
Driven by dearth
To forage for their meat
Even in dooryard bare
And frosty lawn
Under the peril of the human race;
And then one primrose dawn,
Sweet, sweet, O sweet,
And tender, tender,
The bluebirds woke the happy earth
With song.

Katharine Lee Bates

JOY

My heart is like a little bird
That sits and sings for very gladness.
Sorrow is some forgotten word,
And so, except in rhyme, is sadness.
The world is very fair to me
Such azure skies, such golden weather,
I'm like a long caged bird set free,
My heart is lighter than a feather.
I rise rejoicing in my life;
I live with love of God and neighbor;
My days flow on unmarred by strife,
And sweetened by my pleasant labor.
O youth! O spring! O happy days,
Ye are so passing sweet, and tender,
And while the fleeting season stays,
I revel care-free, in its splendor.

Ella Wheeler Wilcox

THE SPARROW

Glad to see you, little bird;
'Twas your little chirp I heard
What did you intend to say?
Give me something this cold day?

That I will, and plenty, too;
All the crumbs I saved for you.
Don't be frightened—here's a treat
I will wait and see you eat.

Shocking tales I hear of you;
Chirp, and tell me, are they true?
Robbing all the summer long;
Don't you think it very wrong?

Thomas says you steal his wheat;
John complains, his plums you eat—
Choose the ripest for your share,
Never asking whose they are.

But I will not try to know
What you did so long ago
There's your breakfast, eat away;
Come to see me every day.

Anonymous

THE FIRST BIRD O' SPRING

Winter on Mount Shasta,
April down below;
Golden hours of glowing sun
Sudden showers of snow!
Under leafless thickets
Early wild-flowers cling;
But, oh, my dear, I'm fain to hear
The first bird o' Spring!
Alders are in tassel,
Maples are in bud;
Waters of the blue McCloud
Shout in joyful flood;
Through the giant pine-trees
Flutters many a wing;
But, oh, my dear, I long to hear
The first bird o' Spring!
Candle-light and fire-light
Mingle at the Bend;
'Neath the roof of Bo-hai-pan
Light and shadow blend.
Sweeter than a wood-thrush
A maid begins to sing;
And, oh, my dear, I'm glad to hear
The first bird o' Spring!

Henry Van Dyke

THE SKYLARK

The earth was green, the sky was blue
I saw and heard one sunny morn,
A skylark hang between the two,
A singing speck above the corn;

A stage below, in gay accord,
White butterflies danced on the wing,
And still the singing skylark soared,
And silent sank and soared to sing.

The cornfield stretched a tender green
To right and left beside my walks;
I knew he had a nest unseen
Somewhere among the million stalks

And as I paused to hear his song,
While swift the sunny moments slid,
Perhaps his mate sat listening long,
And listened longer than I did.

Christina Georgina Rossetti

FLUTTER, LITTLE BIRD

Observe the loving mother bird,
Up in the spreading tree,

Correct with stern but loving word,
Her tender chickadee.

The feathered youngster tries to flap
His embryonic wings,

While mother cheers the little chap,
As to the bough he clings.

He makes a most heroic jump,
Alas, it is in vain,

She says,'Don't mind a little bump',
Just try it once again.

Flutter, little bird and keep on trying,
By and by you will be flying;

You can do it, take my word,
Keep on fluttering, little bird.

George Ade

THE END OF SUMMER

The birds laugh loud and long together
When Fashion's followers speed away
At the first cool breath of autumn weather.
Why, this is the time, cry the birds, to stay!

When the deep calm sea and the deep sky over
Both look their passion through sun-kissed space,
As a blue-eyed maid and her blue-eyed lover
Might each gaze into the other's face.

Oh! this is the time when careful spying
Discovers the secrets Nature knows.
You find when the butterflies plan for flying
Before the thrush or the blackbird goes ,

You see some day by the water's edges
A brilliant border of red and black;
And then off over the hills and hedges
It flutters away on the summer's track.

The shy little sumacs, in lonely places,
Bowed all summer with dust and heat,
Like clean-clad children with rain-washed faces,
Are dressed in scarlet from head to feet.

Ella Wheeler Wilcox

HIGH FLIGHT

Oh! I have slipped the surly bonds of Earth
And danced the skies on laughter-silvered wings;
Sunward I've climbed, and joined the tumbling mirth
Of sun-split clouds, and done a hundred things
You have not dreamed of wheeled and soared and swung
High in the sunlit silence. Hovering there,
I ve chased the shouting wind along, and flung
My eager craft through footless halls of air

Up, up the long, delirious burning blue
I ve topped the wind-swept heights with easy grace
Where never lark, or ever eagle flew
And, while with silent, lifting mind I've trod
The high untrespassed sanctity of space,
Put out my hand, and touched the face of God.

John Gillespie Magee

BIRD SONG

The Robin sings of willow-buds,
Of snowflakes on the green;
The bluebird sings of Mayflowers,
The crackling leaves between;
The veery has a thousand tales
To tell to girl and boy;
But the oriole, the oriole,
Sings, 'Joy! joy! joy!'

The pewee calls his little mate,
Sweet Phoebe, gone astray,
The warbler sings,
What fun, what fun,
To tilt upon the spray!
The cuckoo has no song, but clucks,
Like any wooden toy;
But the oriole, the oriole,
Sings, 'Joy! joy! joy!'

The grosbeak sings the rose's birth,
And paints her on his breast;
The sparrow sings of speckled eggs,
Soft brooded in the nest.
The wood-thrush sings of peace,
Sweet peace, Sweet peace, without alloy;
But the oriole, the oriole,
Sings, 'Joy! joy! joy!'

Laura Elizabeth Howe Richards

THE SANDPIPER

Across the lonely beach we flit,
One little sandpiper and I,
And fast I gather, bit by bit,
The scattered driftwood, bleached and dry
The wild waves reach their hands for it,
The wild wind raves, the tide runs high,
As up and down the beach we flit,
One little sandpiper and I.

I watch him as he skims along,
Uttering his sweet and mournful cry;
He starts not at my fitful song,
Nor flash of fluttering drapery.
He has no thought of any wrong,
He scans me with a fearless eye;
Stanch friends are we, well tried and strong,
The little sandpiper and I.

Comrade, where wilt thou be to-night,
When the loosed storm breaks furiously?
My driftwood fire will burn so bright!
To what warm shelter canst thou fly?
I do not fear for thee, though wroth
The tempest rushes through the sky;
For are we not God's children both,
Thou, little sandpiper, and I?

Celia Thaxter

THE HUMMING-BIRD

Voyager on golden air,

Type of all that 's fleet and fair,

Incarnate gem,

Live diadem!

Stay, forget lost Paradise,

Star-bird fallen from happy skies. —

Vanished! Earth is not his home.

Onward, onward must he roam,

Swift passion-thought,

In rapture wrought;

Issue of the soul's desire,

Plumed with beauty and with fire.

John Vance Cheney

WINGS OF A DOVE

At sunset, when the rosy light was dying
Far down the pathway of the west,
I saw a lonely dove in silence flying,
To be at rest.

Pilgrim of air, I cried, could I but borrow
Thy wandering wings, thy freedom blest,
I'd fly away from every careful sorrow,
And find my rest.

But when the filmy veil of dusk was falling,
Home flew the dove to seek his nest,
Deep in the forest where his mate was calling
To love and rest.

Peace, heart of mine!
No longer sigh to wander;
Lose not thy life in barren quest.
There are no happy islands over yonder;
Come home and rest.

Henry Van Dyke

HAUSSPERLING·*Passer domesticus* (L)

THE SPARROW

A little bird, with plumage brown,
Beside my window flutters down,
A moment chirps its little strain,
Then taps upon my window-pane,
And chirps again, and hops along,
To call my notice to its song;
But I work on, nor heed its lay,
Till, in neglect, it flies away.

So birds of peace and hope and love
Come fluttering earthward from above,
To settle on life's window-sills,
And ease our load of earthly ills;
But we, in traffic's rush and din
Too deep engaged to let them in,
With deadened heart and sense plod on,
Nor know our loss till they are gone.

Paul Laurence Dunbar

THE BLUE JAY

No brigadier throughout the year
So civic as the jay.
A neighbor and a warrior too,
With shrill felicity

Pursuing winds that censure us
A February day,
The brother of the universe
Was never blown away.

The snow and he are intimate;
I 've often seen them play
When heaven looked upon us all
With such severity,

I felt apology were due
To an insulted sky,
Whose pompous frown was nutriment
To their temerity.

The pillow of this daring head Is
pungent evergreens;
His larder — terse and militant —
Unknown, refreshing things;

His character a tonic,
His future a dispute;
Unfair an immortality
That leaves this neighbor out.

Emily Dickinson

BIRD'S NESTS

The skylark's nest among the grass
And waving corn is found;
The robin's on a shady bank,
With oak leaves strewn around.

The wren builds in an ivied thorn,
Or old and ruined wall;
The mossy nest, so covered in,
You scarce can see at all.

The martins build their nests of clay,
In rows beneath the eaves;
While silvery lichens, moss and hair,
The chaffinch interweaves.

The sparrow has a nest of hay,
With feathers warmly lined;
The ring-dove's careless nest of sticks
On lofty trees we find.

The blackbird's nest of grass and mud
In brush and bank is found;
The lapwing's darkly spotted eggs
Are laid upon the ground.

Some very neat and beautiful,
Some easily designed.
The habits of each little bird,
And all its patient skill,
Are surely taught by God Himself
And ordered by His will.

Anonymous

Made in the USA
Columbia, SC
19 August 2021

AZTECS

CONQUEST AND GLORY

First published in Australia and New Zealand in 2013 by
Te Papa Press, PO Box 467, Wellington, New Zealand
© Museum of New Zealand Te Papa Tongarewa

Introduction and photographs of objects
© Instituto Nacional de Antropología e Historia
(National Institute of Anthropology and History), Mexico

TE PAPA® is the trademark of the
Museum of New Zealand Te Papa Tongarewa
Te Papa Press is an imprint of the
Museum of New Zealand Te Papa Tongarewa

A catalogue record for this book is available from
the National Library of New Zealand
ISBN 978-0-9876688-3-7

Written by Kerry Jimson
Designed and typeset by Vida & Luke Kelly
Digital imaging by Jeremy Glyde
Printed by Printlink, Wellington

Published in conjuction with the exhibition *Aztecs*, developed in a
partnership between the Museum of New Zealand Te Papa Tongarewa,
Australian Museum, and Museum Victoria.

Te Papa   28 September 2013 – 9 February 2014
Museum Victoria   4 April 2014 – 10 August 2014
Australian Museum   13 September 2014 – 1 February 2015

Museum of New Zealand Te Papa Tongarewa acknowledges and thanks
Instituto Nacional de Antropología e Historia (INAH).

SECRETARÍA DE
EDUCACIÓN PÚBLICA

CONTENTS

INTRODUCTION

In the first half of the 16th century, the Spanish captain Hernán Cortés and his forces arrived to the territory known today as Mesoamerica. The Mexica Empire, better known as the Aztec Empire, was the most powerful society of the time, its domains extending beyond the southern Mexican border and into Central America.

Legend has it that various groups of people, known as Chichimecas (barbarians), left the mythical island of Aztlán in search of a place to settle. The Aztecs were the last of the Chichimecas. After a long migration, they finally settled on an island in Lake Texcoco, where they believed they had found the sign sent to them by their guardian god, Huitzilopochtli: an eagle perched on a cactus eating a snake. This sacred symbol, indicating the place where they should live, gave rise to the city of Tenochtitlán in the year 1325.

The Aztecs were an imperialist society. In 1428, to free themselves from the dominant Tepaneca people, they joined forces with the cities of Texcoco and Tlacopan to form the Triple Alliance. From this point, the Aztec Empire grew rapidly, first overpowering the coastal towns of Lake Texcoco and then conquering much of Mesoamerica. The goal was to implement a tax system that would support the growing city of Tenochtitlán and its allies.

A great variety of food products, objects of stone, shell, wooden masks, metal, textiles, and exotic animals, among other materials, were sent as tax by the conquered regions. These were mainly used to support the government and military, but large amounts were also stored as precautionary measures against famines caused by droughts.

The Aztec Empire lasted about 200 years, during which time the Aztecs managed to extend their rule over a vast territory and took control of around 400 towns.

The Aztec social structure was simple and mainly based on family ties. *Calpulli* (neighbourhoods) were family collectives engaged in similar work and loyal to the same patron god. It was in these neighbourhoods that merchants and craftsmen lived. Each *calpulli* was headed by a noble who was responsible for controlling production and receiving the tax that would later be sent to the Triple Alliance.

Religion and world view were inseparable components of Aztec life. Military conquests were made in the name of the guardian god Huitzilopochtli (god of war). An elaborate calendar governed life and various gods presided over every celebration and activity.

For the Aztecs, the Earth was the centre of the universe. Above it were 13 heavens where the gods and heavenly bodies lived. Below was the underworld, governed by Mictlantecuhtli (god of death and lord of the underworld), and divided into nine levels, all inhabited by various forces.

Aztec life was strongly linked to myths. Myths justified Aztec existence, dominance, and the practice of human sacrifice during celebrations. According to the creation myth, the world had been created four times, and destroyed by cataclysms each time. It was therefore necessary to create a Fifth Sun (the era in which we now live). The gods gathered for this purpose. One sacrificed himself in a fire and became the sun. Another followed and became the moon. Finally, all the gods sacrificed themselves so that the sun and stars would be able to move through sky and there would be days and nights.

The Aztecs' sacrifices of human hearts and blood were to nourish the sun's movement and, thereby, ensure the continuation of life itself.

Today, the legacy of the Aztecs lives on. The sacred sign of the eagle perched on a cactus is Mexico's national emblem and lies at the centre of Mexico's cultural identity.

Raúl Barrera
Curator, Instituto Nacional de Antropología e Historia
(National Institute of Anthropology and History), Mexico

JOURNEY TO THE CENTRE OF THE UNIVERSE

After eight relentless months of siege, the proud and warrior-like people of the great city of Tenochtitlán were starving – reduced to eating bark and worms. Their supply of fresh water had long since been cut off. Deadly smallpox had laid waste to one in four.

Cannon ball attacks had flattened their sacred temples. Still the Aztecs refused to surrender. Perhaps they knew what their fate would be when their fierce and bitter enemies, the Tlaxcalans, entered their beloved city. To die fighting was a noble and sacred death . . .

Though the Aztec Empire fell, the Aztec people survived. Their descendants live on today in Mexico. Excavations for public works in Mexico City unearthed the remains of the Huey Teocalli (Great Temple), commonly referred to as the Templo Mayor. The relics that archaeologists find within and around this temple include elaborate stone carvings, offerings of precious turquoise, jade and gold, and dramatic statues of gods, along with objects from everyday life. These reveal the Aztecs as a sophisticated people who held complex beliefs, used intricate rituals, and were ruled by a powerful elite of nobles and priests. As impressive sculptures and objects of great importance are brought to light, the magnificence of the Aztec empire rises once more.

THE JOURNEY BEGINS

Where did the Aztecs come from? The stories in codices – Aztec manuscripts of picture writing (glyphs) that recorded their history and day-to-day life – say that they came from Aztlán. The word Aztec originally meant 'people from Aztlán'. No one knows the location of Aztlán and historians are uncertain if it actually existed. Archaeological discoveries and the spread of languages suggest that the ancestors of Aztecs came from far north of present-day Mexico. Languages in the same family as Nahuatl, the Aztec language, are found in northern Mexico and as far north as the western United States.

Remnants of the city at the centre of the Aztec empire, Tenochtitlán, surface every day in Mexico City.

Another migration story says the Aztecs came from Chicomoztoc – seven caves located close by Aztlán. Each of the caves held one of the tribes that would eventually settle in the Valley of Mexico – the Xochimilca, Tepaneca, Alcohua, Tlalhuica, Tlaxcalteca, Matlatzinca, and Aztecs. They all spoke the same language and worshipped the same gods. The Aztecs were the last to leave this legendary homeland.

The Aztecs were probably driven to migrate by starvation. Drought may have caused the failure of their main crop, maize. When rains don't fall, the ground bakes and crops wilt in the ground. Maize was cultivated domestically around 9,000 years ago, and turned wandering bands of hunter-gatherers into farmers. But the stable life of agricultural settlements could still change. Starvation had moved populations before.

The Aztecs' principal god, Huitzilopochtli, a god of war who also became associated with the sun, spoke through the dreams and visions of priests to tell them they must search for a new home.

Some time after 1000CE, the Aztecs began their epic journey. They became nomads once more – hunting and foraging to live. Four *teomamaque* (god carriers) led the migration. These priests had the vital task of carrying the sacred relics and holy representations of the gods. The *teomamaque* walked in front of the main group, conversing with the gods and receiving prophecies and visions to guide them.

The Aztecs would wander without a home for over 200 years. One day they roamed into the largest expanse of flat land in the central Mexican highlands, the Valley of Mexico. When they arrived nearly all the best land was occupied, but no single group or person ruled the valley at this time. Instead, separate tribes, city states, and small confederations muscled up against each other. They traded and intermarried. And, in order to gain more resources, such as food and land, they fought.

According to a Spanish friar and historian, the Aztecs settled at Coatépec (snake mountain), on the edge of the Valley of Mexico, for 28 years. There they dammed a river to form a lake, and the land produced rich and plentiful crops. In one version of their myths, Coatépec was the birthplace of the Aztecs' principal god, Huitzilopochtli (god of war). Some of the Aztecs wanted to settle here, but this angered their mighty god. It is written that Huitzilopochtli came down from the mountain top and commanded them to leave.

They resumed their search, marching to Chapultepec (grasshopper hill) on the shore of Lake Texcoco, attracted by the springs there with their fresh, clear water. But the Tepanec people ruled this area, and the Aztecs hadn't asked their permission to stay. The Tepanecs attacked and drove them out.

Their next destination was Culhuacan. The local king allowed them to settle in a region called Tizápan. The Aztecs wielded their fierce fighting skills as paid warriors for the king, who they thought was of Toltec ancestry, and therefore of the highest nobility. The Aztecs revered Toltec culture and accomplishments, especially the great pyramid at Tula, the former Toltec capital.

This heart is made out of jade, a prized material for the Aztecs. In the Aztec myth of the founding of Tenochtitlán, the heart of Copil, Huitzilopochtli's nephew, was ripped out during a mythical battle at Chapultepec and thrown onto the island in Lake Texcoco.

They wanted to connect themselves to the Culhuacan king, so that they would be linked to the ancestors of the auspicious Toltecs. Then the Aztecs' status would rise and their prestige would be indisputable. They asked if one of the king's daughters could marry their god Huitzilopochtli and rule over them as their queen. The king agreed.

One version of this story tells how the Aztecs welcomed the princess with jubilant celebrations. Some time later, they invited the Culhuacan king to visit his daughter. However, when he arrived the king was greeted by a priest wearing his daughter's skin. The god Huitzilopochtli, the priests divined, had identified the princess as a woman who would bring trouble to the Aztecs. He ordered her death and she had been sacrificed. Her skin was then carefully sliced from her corpse, so that it formed a single sheet. To complete the ritual, the priest wore this like a bodysuit, with the skin from the woman's face over his own face.

The Aztecs wandered for over 200 years from their legendary homeland to settle in the Valley of Mexico.

A VISION REALISED

Huitzilopochtli's warning, unsurprisingly, came true – trouble did follow. The incensed Culhuacan king attacked with his army, and a furious, bloody battle raged. He forced the Aztecs into the marshes of Lake Texcoco, where they stood their ground on an island in the lake. The priests then received a vivid prophecy from Huitzilopochtli. They must settle in the place where they saw an eagle perched on a prickly pear cactus. On the swampy land, their leaders witnessed this exact vision. They wept for joy on seeing the promise of their deliverance. The Aztecs held off the Culhua warriors, and established their homeland. They named it Tenochtitlán, after their leader Tenoch who had delivered them to the spot. The year was 1325.

They built the Huey Teocalli (Great Temple) on the precise place where the eagle was seen on the cactus. They had roamed for centuries and covered great distances to please their god. Now they not only had found their home, they had arrived at the centre of the universe, marked by the spot where the eagle perched on the cactus. From here, they believed, you could rise into the 13 levels of heaven or go down into the nine levels of the underworld.

Before the vision of the eagle on the cactus was seen, the Aztecs witnessed another important sign. On the island in Lake Texcoco, they saw a white juniper tree. At the foot of the tree, a spring of red and a spring of blue flowed from two rocks. All the plants and animals around the springs were white. Huitzilopochtli told the priests that they would see a further sign in this location – an eagle on the cactus. This version had the eagle clutching a bird with resplendent feathers.

The founding legend of Tenochtitlán gave the Aztecs a powerful sense of destiny. The prophecy had also foretold that the Aztecs would win their home in war, and they gained a reputation for having a fearless spirit. The descendants of the Aztecs still take pride in this story. The imagery of the prophecy is widely reproduced in modern Mexico and features prominently on the Mexican flag.

By settling on the island in Lake Texcoco the Aztecs were again in the region of the Tepanecs, and they became the subjects of the Tepanec king, who lived in his city stronghold of Azcapotzalco. The Aztecs acted as his mercenaries (soldiers for a foreign army) and paid him tribute (tax), which was usually of food, such as legumes, maize, chillies, beans, and squash.

THE GOLDEN EAGLE

This *águila cuauhxicalli* (eagle vessel) held the blood and hearts of sacrificial victims.

Eagles were an important symbol for the Aztecs. They associated the high-flying and courageous bird with the sun. The eagle warriors were an elite fighting force. The receptacles that held the blood and hearts of sacrificial victims, called *cuauhxicalli*, were often eagle-shaped. These sacrifices were to nourish the sun.

The golden eagle is the bird to which the Aztecs referred in their prophecy. This impressive bird of prey is found throughout much of the northern hemisphere. Its wingspan is as wide as a grown man is tall. It is capable of taking down ground predators much larger than itself. On an attack run it can reach speeds of up to 240 kilometres per hour.

After the Aztecs established Tenochtitlán on the island in Lake Texcoco, they would go on to conquer much of the wide strip of land that joins North and South America. Many civilisations rose and fell in this area before the Aztec Empire blazed briefly and brightly. The Mayans, Zapotecs, Olmecs, Toltecs, and Teotihuacáns had all developed rich, dominant cultures there. Like the Aztecs would, they had built stepped pyramids, sacrificed humans, and used a complex system of calendars.

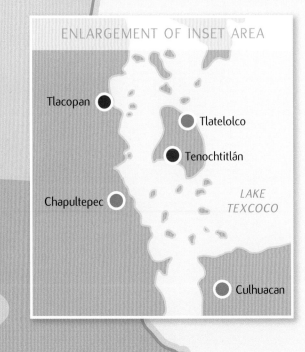

ENLARGEMENT OF INSET AREA

Tlacopan

Tlatelolco

Tenochtitlán

Chapultepec

LAKE TEXCOCO

Culhuacan

Aztec Empire
(at the time of
Spanish arrival)

Triple Alliance cities
(Tenochtitlán,
Tlacopan, Texcoco)

Other cities

Tula

Tlaxcala

Teotihuacán

Texcoco

Veracruz

Coatépec

Cholula

WORLD VIEW

Mexico

AZTEC, MEXICA, OR TENOCHCA?

The people known today as Aztecs actually had three names for themselves in Nahuatl, their original language: Aztecs, Mexicas, and Tenochcas.

AZTEC means people from Aztlán, their legendary homeland. Prussian geographer and naturalist Alexander von Humboldt coined the modern usage of 'Aztecs' in 1810. The term now refers generally to the people inhabiting the Valley of Mexico during the 15th and 16th centuries, and specifically to the Nahuatl-speaking people who built Tenochtitlán.

MEXICA is thought to come from the word Mexi, a secret name for the Aztecs' principal god, Huitzilopochtli (god of war). According to a Spanish chronicler, Huitzilopochtli himself insisted on them adopting this name during their migration: 'You will no longer be called Aztecs: you will be Mexica.'

TENOCHCA comes from Tenoch, the leader who delivered the Aztecs to their new home on the island of Texcoco.

The imagery of the prophecy that led the Aztecs to establish the great city Tenochtitlán is depicted everywhere in Mexico today. It features on the Mexican flag (above) and is proudly reproduced elsewhere.

DECODING THE CODICES

The glyphs — the individual pictures — that make up the 'writing' of the Aztecs are like miniature works of art. Some are literal in what they represent, and others require knowledge of Aztec history or culture to understand their meaning.

Footprints mean movement, such as walking, or a path that has been taken.

This hollow spiral means speech, song, or noise. These speech hollows are usually shown in front of a person's mouth, indicating that they are making a sound.

Specific people are indicated by a 'name' picture attached to their back. This person was the first *huey tlatoani* of the Aztecs, Acamapichtli. He was known as 'handful of reeds'.

These swirling currents and eddies represent water.

This is a glyph of a snowstorm — the figure overcome in the centre showing its deadly effects.

These are stars, literally depicted as the 'night's eyes'.

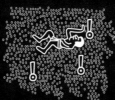

This is how the Aztecs wrote 'eclipse'. It is a sun disk, but has a piece broken out of it.

This sinuous, serpent-like image is a comet.

A creature eating crops indicates plague.

This distressing image is famine — evoking the stomach cramps caused by starvation.

A fertile year is shown with a healthy, flowering plant.

This is the mat of power, which was sat on by the great ruler.

This is the glyph of war — a shield with four darts behind it. The Aztecs hurled darts using slings.

This burning temple signifies conquest.

This shape represents a place.

THE AZTECS SPLIT IN TWO

In 1337, disputes over land saw a group of Aztecs split off from the main city. They formed a new city, Tlatelolco, which competed with Tenochtitlán for power. Both cities fought for the Tepanec king of Azcapotzalco. They conquered city states, increasing the wealth and size of the Tepanec kingdom.

The Aztecs wanted a king of their own and again sought a princess to marry from a Culhuacan king. Through either good diplomacy or their grown stature, they persuaded the king to agree. In 1375, one of his princesses married an Aztec noble and they had a son, Acamapichtli. He became the first Aztec *huey tlatoani* (literally meaning 'great speaker', but also meaning 'great leader').

In 1428, the Tepanec king bestowed land on the Aztecs for their mercenary services. It wasn't unusual for kings to grant territory to powerful warlords. Now the Aztecs had lands that paid them a tribute.

A prickly pear cactus glyph stands for Tenochtitlán – the place where the prophecy was realised.

A round earth mound is the glyph for the city of Tlatelolco. After disputes over land, a group of Aztecs split off from Tenochtitlán and established this rival city on a nearby sandy bank of the island.

As the years passed, rivalry between Tenochtitlán and Tlatelolco intensified. Tlatelolco had prospered, becoming the main market and trading post for the area. As it grew in wealth and power, Tlatelolco vied for dominance with Tenochtitlán. Although warriors from Tenochtitlán and Tlatelolco fought side by side with the Tepanecs, occasionally they fought each other. (Eventually, in 1473, Tenochtitlán would attack and overrun Tlatelolco, and the *huey tlatoani* at the time, Axayacatl, installed a governor in the defeated city.)

THE SEEDS OF EMPIRE

From 1371, the Tepanec king Tezozomoc was able to vastly expand his dominion with the two Aztec cities fighting by his side. One of his daughters married the second Aztec *huey tlatoani*, Huitzilihuitl, and their son, Chimalpopoca, became the third *huey tlatoani* of Tenochtitlán in 1417, though he was just a child.

In 1426, Tezozomoc died. After the death of this powerful ruler, rivalry exploded between the potential heirs to his throne. The late Tepanec king had wanted his son Tayauh to be the next king. But Tayauh's brother, Maxtla, murdered him and seized the throne.

This had a direct, deadly effect on the *huey tlatoani* of Tenochtitlán because Chimalpopoca had supported Tayauh's bid for power. It's likely Maxtla had Chimalpopoca assassinated, although some sources say Chimalpopoca was imprisoned by Maxtla and hanged himself, a noble way to die for the Aztecs.

Snuffing out the opposition wasn't out of character for Tepanec leaders. Maxtla's father

Tezozomoc had also dealt ruthlessly with the leaders of the cities he had overrun. He had done exactly this with the help of the Aztecs when he sacked the city state of Texcoco. To quell any future threats from the leadership, he killed the king of Texcoco. He then gave Texcoco to Tenochtitlán as a reward.

But Tezozomoc didn't quite get what he wanted by slaying the king of Texcoco. Opposition lived on in the king's son, Nezahualcoyotl, who had escaped the attack. And Nezahualcoyotl had formidable allies: he was the nephew of the new *huey tlatoani* of Tenochtitlán, Itzcoatl, who had replaced his murdered nephew (some sources say brother). Rebellion was in the air. Besides his lineage, Itzcoatl had a reputation as a dynamic and forceful leader in battle, which aided his selection as *huey tlatoani* as the threat of war with the Tepanecs grew.

Itzcoatl enlisted the help of Nezahualcoyotl, and what forces he could muster in Texcoco. The Tepanec king of the state of Tlacopan also joined them – his state was already in conflict with the rest of the confederation. The three kings went into battle against Maxtla and dealt him a devastating defeat in the Tepanec capital, Azcapotzalco. Nezahualcoyotl then became the king of Texcoco.

This is how the Aztec Empire began to take shape. First it was an alliance between three different cities – Tenochtitlán, Texcoco, and Tlacopan. The three rulers divided the land between them.

The Tepanec rulers within the territory weren't punished or stripped of power – they were invited back from where they had fled and made allies. Local nobles were given land and key roles to keep them loyal to the alliance. Prime land in the new territories was given to high-ranking Aztec officials.

This method was unlike the Tepanec strategy of killing or banishing conquered kings, but had been used successfully elsewhere in the Valley of Mexico. It became the pattern for further expansion by the Triple Alliance.

The commoners in the conquered land now worked for the growing empire. The leaders had been brought on side. Military might and savvy diplomacy became hallmarks of the Aztec expansion – as would dread at the lethal consequences of opposing them.

Codex Tellerian-Remensis shows one version of the death of Chimalpopoca, the third *huey tlatoani* of Tenochtitlán. The Tepanec ruler Maxtla recruited a warrior from Tlatelolco to assassinate Chimalpopoca in 1426. The murder is shown in the top half, with Chimalpopoca in his burial shroud. A line links Chimalpopoca to his successor, his uncle Itzcoatl.

This vivid image is Nezahualcoyotl on the attack in full battle dress. He wears quilted cotton to protect him from arrows. He is about to strike with a *macuahuitl*, a wooden weapon with edges lined with obsidian, a volcanic glass.

THE RISE AND RISE OF TENOCHTITLÁN

Itzcoatl, the fourth *huey tlatoani* (great leader) of Tenochtitlán, was the obvious choice to command the Triple Alliance from the outset. Nezahualcoyotl, who now ruled Texcoco, looked to his uncle Itzcoatl for guidance in leadership and conquest. The new king of Tlacopan, Totoquihuaztli, owed a debt to Itzcoatl for organising the rebellion. Over successive years, future Aztec leaders would consolidate Itzcoatl's dominance. The *huey tlatoani*'s military bristled with aggression and went on to exert its power over ever more states. As the Aztecs conquered more land, the alliance became less relevant.

Soon after the alliance's first battle, which defeated Maxtla at Azcapolzalco, Itzcoatl attacked Coyoacan, the Tepanec city to which Maxtla had retreated. He did not put Maxtla to death; instead he left the Tepanec king in power. Though this was only a temporary reprieve: three years after the alliance's victory, Nezahualcoyotl tore Maxtla's heart out in a sacrificial killing, avenging his father's murder.

Next the alliance conquered Xochimilco and Culhuacan, then Chalco. The Aztecs overwhelmed all the cities surrounding Lake Texcoco, strengthening their power in the region. Afterward, they moved on to other areas within the Valley of Mexico, such as the Valley of Morelos.

Itzcoatl died in 1440 and Moctezuma I was installed as the fifth *huey tlatoani*. Moctezuma began conquests outside the Valley of Mexico. By the time of the Spanish invasion in 1519, the Aztecs had conquered 360 towns and cities in 38 provinces. Their impressive might reached across 200,000 square kilometres to dominate a population of up to six million people.

The Aztecs weren't always successful in their campaigns. The equally fierce Tarascan people, who lived to the west of Tenochtitlán, had pushed their borders out in similar attacks. When their forces reached the Toluca Valley in the 1470s, the *huey tlatoani* sent a large force to face them. The Aztecs lost the battle. They weren't crushed in defeat, but any idea of expansion to the west was no longer a possibility. Each side built up a fortified defensive zone between their empires.

This sculpture is of a standard bearer. His face sticks out of a helmet shaped like a serpent's head. His left hand would have been used to hold a pole with a banner attached, identifying an order of snake warriors.

STRATEGIC DIPLOMACY

The Aztecs favoured negotiating with states rather than completely defeating them, which made economic and political sense. The existing governments were largely left in place so that the state could still function smoothly and tributes (taxes) start flowing immediately. Commoners were enlisted for military service or as labour for public works in Tenochtitlán. A total defeat would disrupt an easy transition into the Aztec system. An overwhelming military victory could also result in a much greater loss of life than was necessary. Less people would mean less wealth to extract from the conquered state and less victims available for sacrifice. So martial power gave way to diplomacy.

As the empire grew, so did the manpower it could call on for military service. In the field, the Aztecs could often muster an army as large as the population of the city states they sought to conquer. On occasion, the conquered joined the Aztecs in further conquests, then shared in the spoils.

Once conquered, the nobility and kings were invited to Tenochtitlán. There they attended sumptuous feasts and festivities and received lavish gifts. This was all in aid of the Aztec strategy of getting to know their new subjects, and it also ensured the conquered lords got into the habit of deference. It's easy to imagine that they would be impressed by the size, wealth, and power of the city. Even enemies received these invitations, showing how far the Aztecs were willing to take this approach and how sure they were of their power.

The conquered kings and lords were required to give their daily respects to the *huey tlatoani*. They had to attend festivals where sacrifices took place, and where many of the victims were warriors captured in war. So while these conquered nobles received privileged treatment, the fate of those who opposed the Aztecs would have been very clear to them. Military superiority, bloody sacrificial rituals for dissenters, and plentiful wealth and privilege for compliance were powerful incentives to keep the conquered nobility on side.

Along with this psychological intimidation and personal connection, the Aztecs established a handy insurance – the heirs of the lords had to remain in Tenochtitlán until adulthood.

The connections between conquered states and the empire were further strengthened by marriages between the families of the kings. But rebellions were common, especially when the Aztecs demanded excessive tributes. Sometimes 'rebellion' simply meant the king of the state refused to pay his tribute. The Aztecs would then conquer the state again. Some states were conquered several times.

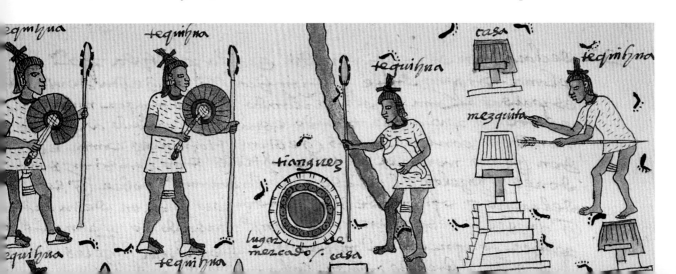

THE PRICE OF WEAKNESS

But the Aztec Empire was not infallible. Tizoc, the seventh *huey tlatoani*, was a weak military leader, causing the Aztec empire to go into a brief decline while he ruled. Several city states rebelled when they realised his short-comings. Tizoc's weak reign demonstrates the potential fragility of the Aztec method of control. No large garrisons of soldiers dwelt in the conquered regions to quell discontent. The Aztecs relied instead on 'friendly' local leaders, whose compliance was induced with wealth and privileges. Added to the appeal of this preferential treatment was the very real threat of the powerful Aztec army marching into town. But when Tizoc's military strategy didn't uphold the fearsome reputation of the army, then cracks appeared in the Aztecs' influence. Why give obedience and pay tribute when the mighty Aztecs can't force you to? When one state rebelled, others followed, starting a chain reaction.

But Tizoc's reign was brief – just five years. He wasn't ill; his death was abrupt and unexpected. Was he poisoned? His brother, Ahuitzotl, a renowned warrior, was probably itching to take the throne. Tizoc's court would have seen how his poor military strategy was weakening the empire. His sudden demise would have been quietly welcomed.

This carving is of an organ pipe cactus. These were often used to mark farm boundaries. A carved boundary marker like this would have been used to signal the boundary between Tenochtitlán and its sister city, Tlatelolco.

Futher detail of Aztec warriors from the Codex Mendoza (left).

FAMILY TREE OF GREAT LEADERS

ACAMAPICHTLI
Reigns 1375–1395
The first Aztec *huey tlatoani*

HUITZILIHUITL
Reigns 1396–1426
The second *huey tlatoani*
He cements relationships
between Aztec nobles and
other nobility in the region.

ITZCOATL
Reigns 1427–1440
The fourth *huey tlatoani*
He forges the Triple Alliance that
eventually dominates the area
today called Mexico.

CHIMALPOPOCA
Reigns 1417–1426
The third *huey tlatoani*
He is assassinated by the Tepanec
king Maxtla for supporting Maxtla's
brother's bid for the Tepanec throne.

MOCTEZUMA I
Reigns 1440–1469
The fifth *huey tlatoani*
He extends Aztec dominance
outside of the Valley of Mexico.

DAUGHTER ———————————— SON

AXAYACATL
Reigns 1469–1481
The sixth *huey tlatoani*
He continues expansion and
overthrows Tenochtitlán's
sister city, Tlatelolco.

TIZOC
Reigns 1481–1486
The seventh *huey tlatoani*
He reigns weakly and dies
mysteriously at a young age.

AHUITZOTL
Reigns 1486–1502
The eighth *huey tlatoani*
He is a formidable warrior
and begins a new campaign
of conquests further afield.

MOCTEZUMA II
Reigns 1502–1520
The ninth *huey tlatoani*
He concentrates his efforts on
consolidating newly gained territory,
until the arrival of the Spanish.

CUITLAUAC
Reigns in 1520
The tenth *huey tlatoani*
He battles the Spanish
conquistadors (conquerors)
but dies of smallpox.

CUAUHTEMOC
Reigns 1520–1521
The eleventh and last *huey tlatoani*
He takes a last stand against the
Spanish, but surrenders on 13
August 1521 and is hanged in 1525.

TRIBUTE AND SACRIFICE

The city state of Tenochtitlán sucked in riches from the areas it had conquered – luxury materials such as jade and turquoise, delicacies and exotic foods, animal skins, feathers of tropical birds, and fine textiles. This powered the economy of the Aztec capital and turned it into a wealthy and opulent cultural centre. Collecting tributes for the Aztecs also stimulated the economies of the conquered city states.

Those who had to bear the final cost of this system were the commoners outside the big city states. They produced the main foods, such as maize and other crops, wove lengths of cloth, and made craft items, such as pottery – and handed over a portion of these as tribute. The Aztecs bartered goods, but also had a currency of cacao beans, lengths of cotton cloth, small copper axe heads, and quills filled with gold.

When the Aztecs made conquests outside of the Valley of Mexico, the tribute consisted of luxury goods that could be more easily carried over such enormous distances; heavy and bulky tributes such as food became impractical and the porters carrying it would eat too much of it before it could be delivered.

The amount of tribute owed to the Aztecs depended on the size of the land conquered and how many people lived there. Human power equalled wealth. The more servants you had, the richer you were because all work required manual labour. Although toys with wheels had been devised, the Aztecs had not translated this technology into machines. They had no carts, and no beasts of burden like horses and oxen.

Aztec nobles wore adornments made of precious materials. This Aztec warrior (left) wears a plug in his lower lip. This lip plug (right), made out of jade and gold, would also have been worn in the lower lip, so that the carving of the bird protruded.

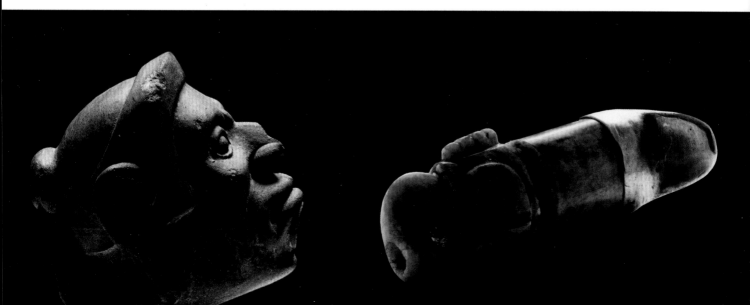

These gold earrings would have been inserted like plugs into the earlobes.

The Aztec goldsmiths attained a high level of craftsmanship, creating beautiful adornments for the nobility from the luxury materials given in tribute — gold, jade, precious stones, and the feathers of tropical birds.

Non-nobles who were well-off could also own these, but could only wear them in private. It was forbidden for commoners to dress lavishly. Instead they could wear simpler items made out of fired clay, wood, or bone.

Few examples of this sort survive from the Aztec era. Most of the gold items were taken by the Spanish and melted down into ingots.

CODEX MENDOZA

The Codex Mendoza displays a fascinating picture of what the tributes entailed. It shows what tribute was due from the 38 provinces the Aztecs once ruled, how often it needed to be paid, the nature of the goods, and the quantities. The Viceroy of New Spain, Antonio de Mendoza, created the codex about 20 years after the fall of the Aztecs. He was living in Mexico City, the name given to Tenochtitlán by the conquering Spaniards, and made the codex for his monarch, Charles I of Spain (also known as Charles V, the Holy Roman Emperor).

Mendoza made the codex in the pictographic style of the Aztecs with a commentary in Spanish.

Mendoza despatched the codex from Mexico by ship. French privateers, however, attacked the fleet and the codex came into the possession of the cosmographer for the king of France. It then passed through a number of hands and was eventually deposited in the Bodleian Library at Oxford University in 1659. There the codex remained in obscurity until its rediscovery in 1831.

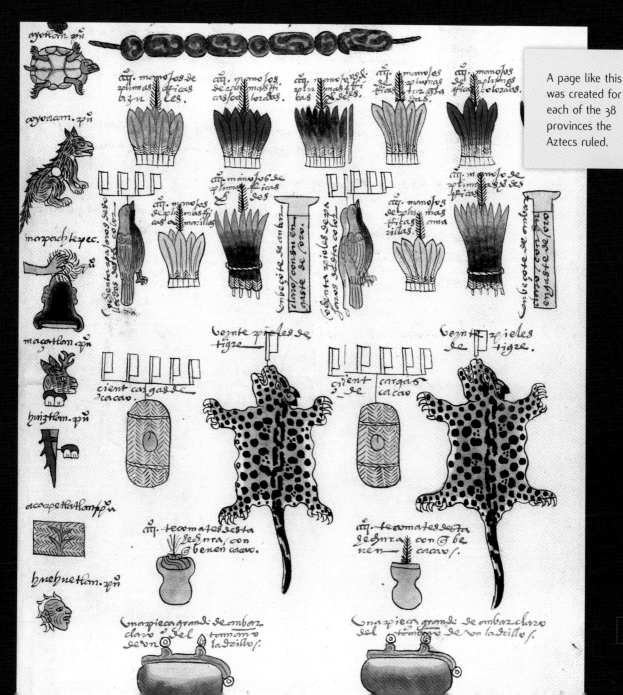

A page like this was created for each of the 38 provinces the Aztecs ruled.

TENOCHTITLÁN

When the Spanish conquistadors arrived in 1519, the thriving metropolis of Tenochtitlán had a population of 150,000 to 200,000, and with its surrounding towns up to 300,000. At this time in history, few cities in the world had topped a population of 100,000. Seville, the largest city in Spain, only had 30,000 people. Tenochtitlán completely dominated the alliance with Tlacopan and Texcoco.

The Spaniards marvelled at Tenochtitlán's size, organisation, liveliness, and beauty — the brilliant painted stone carvings, the vivid hues of nobles' clothes, the splashes of colour in the markets, and the lush green of the gardens. In contrast were 'the temples and oratories of the adjacent cities, built in the form of towers and fortresses, and others on the causeway, all whitewashed, and wonderfully brilliant'.

The city was superbly organised and administered. At the centre, 2 square kilometres had been built

up with rocks and earth to form a solid base. Surrounding this was around 6 square kilometres of family compounds, each with its own *chinampa* (floating garden) for household use. An aqueduct conveyed good drinking water directly to the houses of nobles.

The family compounds could be reached by canoe through a canal system that ran between them. The houses also had drawbridges that connected them to their neighbours. Three great roads, built up over the swampy ground and shallow lake, linked the mainland to the central island. Constant canoe traffic carried goods and food between the mainland and the island.

A large dyke had been built across the lake — in this image it's visible in the water beyond the city. This was put in place after a huge flood devastated the city. Later, engineers added a series of sluice gates to control water levels.

THE PYRAMID
OF POWER

The *huey tlatoani*, the great leader of the Aztecs, was head of the state and the army and acted as the chief priest. His word had to be obeyed. The *huey tlatoani* gained his title through a hereditary bloodline. But his military prowess, political skills, and religious devotion also played a part in his selection.

Moctezuma II, for example, was the nephew of the previous *huey tlatoani*, Ahuitzotl, but he was also a talented general. Aztecs venerated military prowess – it expanded their empire and provided the necessary sacrificial victims needed to maintain the health of the sun and balance within the universe.

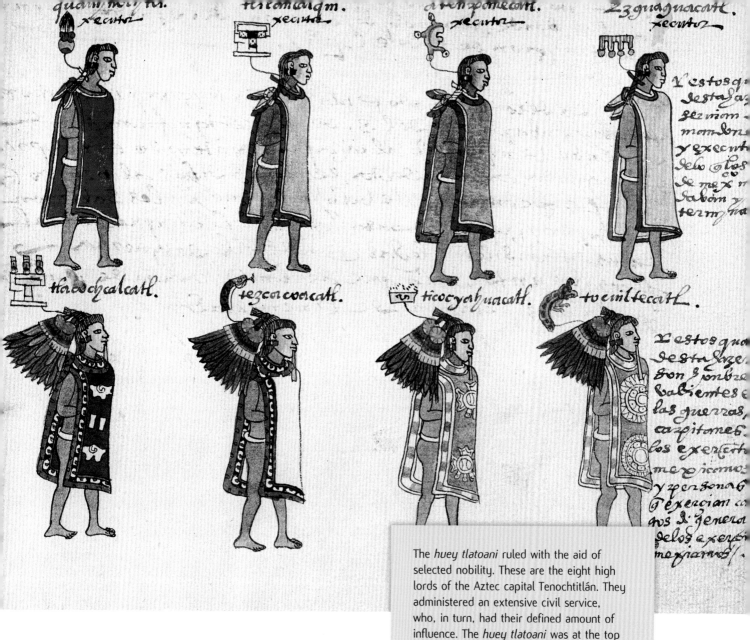

The *huey tlatoani* instructed the city leaders of Tenochtitlán. These leaders formed a kind of senate of the ruling classes. The members of this senate were selected for office by their *calpulli*. In large urban areas, *calpulli* were districts, often occupied by people with the same occupation, but the term originally comes from family groupings.

The Aztec Empire required a dedicated force of well-trained warriors to make it work. But it also required an army of officials, diplomats, judges, accountants, bureaucrats, administrators, and tribute collectors.

This huge civil service made roads and public buildings, dredged canals, cleaned the city, policed markets and vendors, ensured prices remained fair, judged disputes, and punished criminals. Its main function outside of Tenochtitlán revolved around making sure the conquered states complied with their obligations – in other words, that they remained loyal to Tenochtitlán and paid their full tribute.

Moctezuma II, the ninth *huey tlatoani* (left).

The home of the *huey tlatoani* was the heart of the empire. A luxurious complex, it had 100 apartments, each with its own bath, mainly for visitors. Guests could also relax in courtyard gardens and small zoos. It had two judicial courts – one for nobles, one for commoners – and a prison. The residence also contained the administrative centre of government, war council rooms, a hall for the elite eagle warriors, a complex for teachers, and a host of craft workshops – where goldsmiths and jewellers turned the raw materials received as tribute into finely crafted products. The busy complex thronged with people.

A FIRM STRUCTURE

Calpulli were the foundation of Aztec society. They consisted of extended family groupings and usually shared the same occupation. In rural *calpulli*, for example, this would most often be farming. The land wasn't owned by individuals, the *calpulli* owned it collectively. In urban areas, *calpulli* might be made up of crafts-people or tradespeople. They were involved in training, keeping up the high standards of their products, and gained protection for their group's occupation. In this way, they were similar to medieval European guilds.

Cihuacóatl was a goddess, half human, half serpent. The *cihuacóatl* was also an elite position, who carried out the day-to-day running of the empire, acted as the highest judge after the *huey tlatoani*, devised military campaigns, and was head of state when the *huey tlatoani* was away waging war.

Each occupation and each *calpulli* had a patron god. Members gave offerings to their patron. This elaborate ceremonial vessel (right) represents Xilonen, the goddess of young corn.

A *calpulli* would be headed by a *teuctli* (lord). He would appoint a council to make decisions and run the unit.

When enough *calpulli* came together, this created an *altépetl*, a town or city with its own government. Many cities had populations of five to ten thousand. They had temples, palaces for nobles, an armoury, schools, workshops for artisans, a market, and a ball court.

The Aztecs had a structured hierarchy of power. The *calpulli* was ruled by a lord, an *altépetl* was ruled by a higher lord, and the *huey tlatoani* ruled a much grander area of allied city states. This confederation collected tax in the form of a tribute from each *altépetl*. The kings gathered tribute from the lords of each *calpulli*, and the lords collected tribute from the families in their *calpulli*. In this way, tribute flowed up the chain until it reached the Aztec capital.

Social classes also had clear divisions. Two main groups made up the basic class structure. The *pipiltin* were nobles, and the *macehualtin* were free commoners. The *pipiltin* took government, religious, and military positions, and could become *tetecutin* (people holding high military or governmental office). Early in Aztec society, the senior priests and leaders would have formed the nobility. As Aztec society grew, the nobles passed their power on to their children, and classes became more distinct. An individual had to be born into nobility, though a noble could marry a commoner, and their children would be nobles.

You can tell these are figures of commoners because of their short hair. Aztecs didn't allow commoners to have flowing tresses, which would have been seen as ostentatious adornment. Their clothing had to be made out of cloth spun from the coarse fibres of the maguey plant. Commoners caught wearing cotton cloth — a fine material reserved for nobility — could be executed.

Macehualtin worked as farmers, fishers, tradespeople, and craftspeople. Some worked the land owned by nobles. They were free but this status could be taken from them. They could become *tlacotin* (slaves) either through debt – gambling was a common cause – or through punishment for committing a crime. Slaves could work their debt off – or do additional work to earn enough to buy their freedom. Children inherited their parents' original status, not their status as slaves.

A third class existed between nobles and commoners. *Pochtea* were long-distance merchants. They had dual roles. As merchants, they would export obsidian (volcanic glass), jewellery, cochineal (red dye), decorated cloth, and rabbit fur, and import raw materials such as jade, turquoise, shells, tropical bird feathers, and cacao. They also acted as spies. Because they travelled to distant parts of the empire, and through enemy territory, they would hear about political and military events and report these back to Tenochtitlán.

Although little movement existed between social classes, warriors could advance socially. The Aztecs treated highly successful warriors with great respect. If they captured four prisoners for sacrifice, the state would honour them . They could also be given land and become wealthy.

An ordinary slave in the Aztec sense was usually someone who owed a debt. They gave indentured service until the debt had been repaid. Unruly or disobedient slaves, however, became 'wooden-collar slaves', who could be sold and purchased for sacrifice.

SCHOOLED IN YOUR ROLE

Aztec men and women had defined roles, which began early in life. In a ceremony soon after birth, a boy would be given gifts of the tools of his father's occupation. He might also receive weapons. Girls would get gifts of a reed basket, spindle (a device for spinning fibre into thread), and maguey fibre. A girl's umbilical cord would be buried in the home by the hearth and grindstone; a boy's would be buried by a warrior on a battlefield. The Aztecs believed that the qualities a child would have in later life were determined at birth.

Education started at home at the age of three, with the father teaching the boys and the mother teaching the girls. Parents expected their children to work hard. In the case of commoners, girls would learn how to keep the house, spin thread, weave, grind maize, and cook. Boys would learn the basics of their father's profession – for example farming, fishing, or a simple craft.

Elsewhere in the world at this time, formal and higher education were generally restricted to the upper class. But in the Aztec world, everyone went to school – it was compulsory for all classes and for both males and females. There were two main types of schools – the *telpochalli* (a school for commoners) and the *calmecac* (a school for nobles). Occasionally, wealthy children, even if they didn't come from nobility, would be allowed to attend the elite *calmecac*.

EDUCATION
FOR COMMONERS

Commoner children attended the *telpochalli* by the age of 15. Boys learned the fundamentals of religion and history, and of course warfare. They were turned into skilled and hardy fighters. All boys, commoners and nobles alike, had to excel at combat.

A day at a *telpochalli* began at dawn with a cold bath. During the day the boys tended cultivations, repaired temples, and learned how to handle weapons. The severe discipline in these schools implanted the values of service to the community and commitment to the aims of the state. The students were made to practise religious self-sacrifice by puncturing or cutting parts of their bodies. The self-inflicted pain also helped to harden them to the realities of war.

The blue dots in this codex (above) indicate the children's ages. For the three-year-olds, instruction is simple. The older the children become, the more difficult their tasks. The woman on the right is explaining to the girl how to use a spindle – the spinning-top device on the mat. It is used to spin maguey fibre into thread. By the time she is six, the girl is spinning her own thread, and the boy has moved on to more complicated tasks, such as reading symbols.

The thorns of the maguey plant are so sharp that they were used as needles for sewing – and to prick wayward children as punishment.

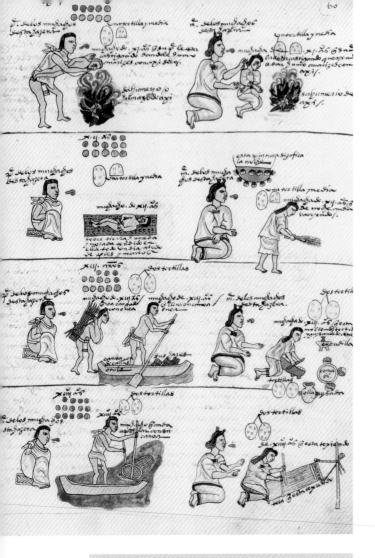

Fathers taught sons and mothers taught daughters. By the time the children are 13 and 14, the boys are transporting large bundles of reeds via canoe, and netting fish; the girls are using the *metlapil* (the mortar, or grinding surface) and *metate* (the pestle, or grinding stick) to grind corn, and, later, a simple loom to weave maguey thread into cloth.

Discipline was harsh for disobedience, poor attitude, or laziness. The children at the top of this image are being made to inhale the stinging fumes of chilli heated on a fire, to sleep on muddy ground, and to sweep the streets at night. Badly behaved children were also pierced with maguey thorns and beaten with sticks.

EDUCATION FOR NOBLES

At age 12 or 13, girls of the nobility would spend a year in a temple. At this point, they could commit themselves to a religious life and become priestesses.

At age 13, noble boys went to a *calmecac* – a boarding school attached to a temple. They learned history, how to govern, and the religious beliefs on which Aztec society was founded. It was made clear to them that they had to be exemplary citizens. This meant living controlled, sober lives. People's behaviour, especially that of nobles, was meant to show decorum and moderation. The priests instructing them would give them religious duties, teach them oral poetry, and astronomy. As in education at home, the work was hard, rules strict, and discipline mercilessly enforced. To instil self-control students were made to fast and given little time to sleep.

Punishments were particularly harsh for boys. This painful discipline helped prepare them for the hardships of war. They learned to endure suffering and have no qualms about inflicting it.

Students at a *calmecac* would be dedicated to a priest-tutor in a temple, emphasising that a person's life and effort needed to be directed toward religious devotion. And religious devotion meant waging war in order to satisfy the gods. This, in turn, drove conquest and expansion. And conquest gave greater power, wealth, and prestige to the Aztec elite. Toward the height of the Aztec Empire, these three concepts appear interchangeable. It's likely the elite also saw the power, wealth, and prestige that the state's military machine brought to them as a religious necessity.

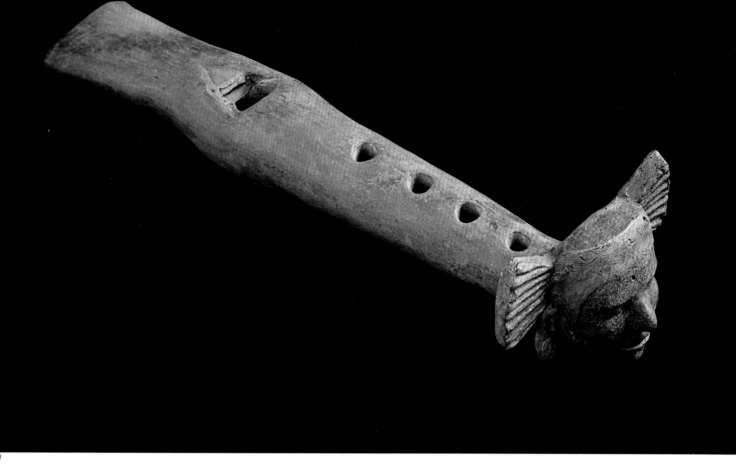

At Aztec festivals, the most commonly played instrument was a clay flute. During the festival of Toxcatl (dedicated to the god Tezcatlipoca), a man dressed as the god played sad melodies on a flute before being sacrificed.

SCHOOL OF PERFORMING ARTS

The religious and military instruction both at home and at school directed subjects to serve the state. The *huey tlatoani* was the ultimate expression of what they were taught. The Aztecs believed he was descended from the gods and an embodiment of the divine warrior. In the person of the *huey tlatoani*, worship and military action fused into a single entity.

One other school existed, the *cuicacalli*. This special school taught musicians, dancers, and performers, who had important roles in religious festivals and celebrations. Singing, music, dancing, pageantry, and drama were essential elements of these public ceremonies. The Aztecs had developed wind instruments that could play several well-defined notes. Musicians composed sophisticated melodies on these instruments.

THE HEART OF THE EMPIRE

Just as Tenochtitlán was the centre the Aztec Empire, the Huey Teocalli (Great Temple), commonly known as the Templo Mayor, was the centre of Tenochtitlán. Its impressive height was visible throughout the city — even from the lake shore. On top of this imposing structure, occupying each half equally, were Huitzilopochtli (god of war), and Tláloc (god of rain and lightning).

The latest Huey Teocalli — it had been rebuilt a number of times — was a remarkable engineering feat. Successive 'editions' had been built on swampy ground over the top of each previous temple and the building therefore needed a huge platform filled with earth and stone to support it. This measured 400 square metres and was 11.5 metres deep. It would have contained over 19,500 cubic metres of fill.

Despite this, the structure needed shoring up with wooden piles. Engineers jammed thousands of these into the base of the temple to stop parts of it from sinking into the ground.

The temple had undergone at least seven rebuilds to commemorate successes in war. Each time, the builders put offerings to the gods into the structure itself. One offering included the remains of 42 children. Their skeletons show no evidence of trauma, and researchers think that the children probably had their throats slit. This is in keeping with historical accounts of sacrifices to Tláloc. The skeletons are believed to date from the 1450s, a time of famine caused by extreme drought.

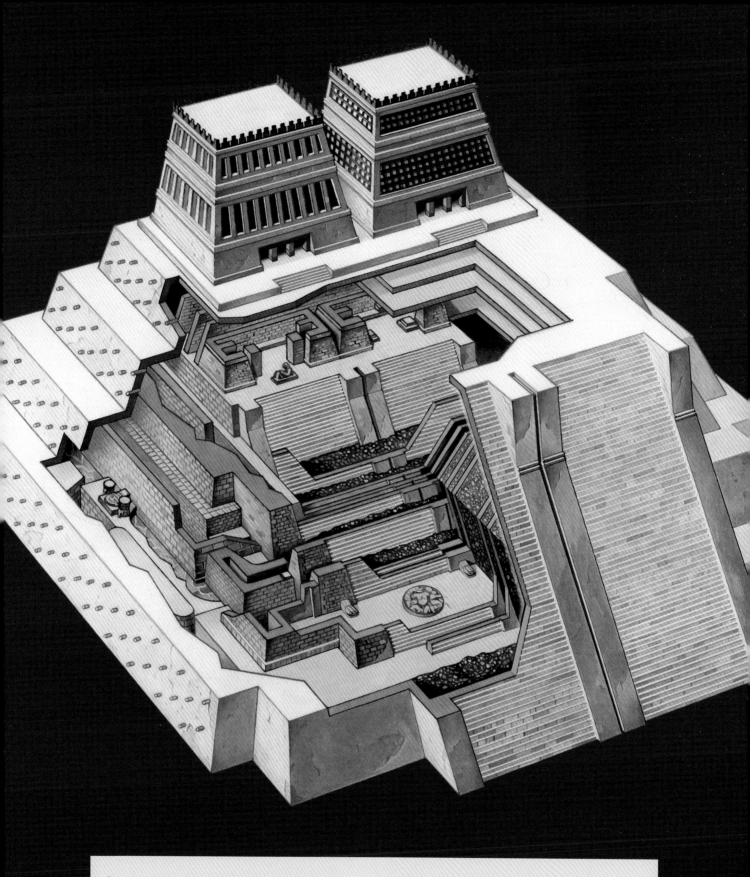

This model of the Huey Teocalli (Great Temple) with its cut-away walls shows the layers of each rebuilding. The first version of the temple was made from earth and wood soon after the founding of the city. Later versions became grander as the size and wealth of the empire increased.

Archaeologists uncovered this offering to Tláloc (god of rain and lightning) in the Huey Teocalli in 2000. The container has been made with volcanic stone and the offerings within it are associated with music, fertility, and plants. Separate layers contained items such as coral, seaweed, sculptures, masks of Tláloc, flutes bearing the image of Xochipilli (god of flowers, nobles, music, and games), knives, and the bones of eagles, herons, and quails.

This is a commemorative stone from the Huey Teocalli (Great Temple). At the top it depicts two of the *huey tlatoque* (great leaders) of Tenochtitlán, the brothers Tizoc and Ahuitzotl, performing a ceremony offering their own blood to Coatlicue (the mother of gods, a goddess of fertility). The blood is on cactus thorns that have been inserted in a ball of straw. The lower part of the stone has the Aztec date that equates to 1487 and refers to the completion date for rebuilding the temple.

THE SYMMETRICAL WORLD

The Aztecs believed that the earthly plane was divided into four equal zones, and the original layout of Tenochtitlán followed this form. The four planes met at a central point where the Huey Teocalli (Great Temple) was built. The point reached up into the levels of heaven and down into the levels of the underworld. Each of the zones had its own direction, god or gods, colour, and symbol. The zones held sway over time, death, fire, water, humans, and the sun. Together they kept the earthly realm in balance.

FLINT KNIFE

NORTH

TEZCATLIPOCA

(god of war and destiny)

BLACK

HOUSE

WEST

QUETZALCÓATL

(god of wind and wisdom)

WHITE

REED

EAST

TONATIUH (sun god)

XIPE TÓTEC (god of spring and renewal)

CAMAXTLI-MIXCOATL (god of hunting)

RED

RABBIT

SOUTH

HUITZILOPOCHTLI

(god of war and the Aztecs' principal god)

BLUE

THE VALLEY
THAT FED A
MILLION PEOPLE

The enterprising Aztecs turned Tenochtitlán from a small, marshy island into a bustling city. It grew to be among the largest in the world at that time, with even more people than London and Constantinople. An agricultural revolution underpinned this extraordinary accomplishment. Human power equalled wealth, but a growing population required greater food production. Maize, which had been domesticated for thousands of years, helped feed the Aztecs. They also had a remarkable technique for turning swampy land and flood plains into fertile gardens: *chinampas*.

Chinampas are raised garden beds. They were made with cane holding-walls that were filled with the mud dredged from the bottom of Lake Texcoco. Farmers planted trees along the edges of the walls to stabilise the sides, and throughout the beds to help anchor them. It was a very labour-intensive activity – both in terms of construction and maintenance, which involved the continual dredging of sediments and aquatic weeds to fertilise the gardens. But the system used very little space and created an abundance of produce. The Aztecs got more out of their land by using crop rotation and adding household organic scraps and human waste to the beds. This latter 'compost' was gathered in the cities then transported by canoe to the *chinampas*.

The large-scale gardening gives us an idea of the Aztecs' sophisticated organisational skills and their keen understanding of the produce they grew.

Perhaps half the food the inhabitants of the Aztec capital ate came from *chinampas*. The Aztecs had their most extensive *chinampas* in Lake Chalco-Xochimilco – essentially the southern area of Lake Texcoco – and this became one of the most productive parts of the Valley of Mexico.

Farmers grew an extraordinary range and quantity of produce on the *chinampas*. An advantage of these beds was that they could grow produce the year round – providing up to seven crops annually. Tomatoes, chilli peppers, squash, maize, beans, and amaranth, among other things, sprang out of the fertile beds. (Amaranth is a plant that produces a large seed head, and the seeds were used in a similar way to grain.) The Aztecs also grew an array of colourful flowers, which were used in festivals and as everyday decoration.

This sculpture depicts a goddess of agriculture. Her outstretched hands would have held symbols of the elements of life over which she presided — flowers or cobs of maize — which connected her to cultivation, growth, and fertility. Farmers prayed and made offerings to such goddesses.

Well into the 20th century, the canals with *chinampas* were a flurry of activity. The growth of Mexico City caused their decline.

A man paddles a *trajinera* (flat-bottomed boat) along a canal in Xochimilco, Mexico. Only a vestige of the canals and *chinampas* remain today.

A canal system, complete with drainage canals, sluice gates, and dykes, was created so the farmers could paddle between the *chinampas* to tend their crops. Water levels could be adjusted as needed. The canals also allowed traders and farmers to transport produce to local markets. And the same canals were used to bring crafts and pottery from the urban areas back to the farms. Large and heavy loads were much easier to move by canal than hauling goods overland.

HARD LABOUR

Farming was hard work. Turning soil, making furrows, and spreading seed were all done by hand, as were harvesting, shucking husks, and removing seeds. Aztec farmers tilled the ground with wooden digging sticks to grow a variety of crops. The rainfall in the Valley of Mexico was unreliable and, unlike the *chinampas*, the ground could be hard and dry. Where possible, farmers used artificial irrigation to ensure the crops grew well.

This piece of the Florentine Codex shows a farmer tilling the soil with a digging stick, then harvesting the resulting crop.

MASSIVE MARKETS

When the Spanish arrived in Tenochtitlán, Moctezuma II showed them around the place and surrounding cities, including the market at Tlatelolco. One of Hernan Cortés's soldiers described what he saw:

> *The noise and bustle of the marketplace below us could be heard almost a league [about 4.2 kilometres] off, and those who had been at Rome and at Constantinople said, that for convenience, regularity, and population they had never seen the like.*
>
> *. . . sweet cooked roots, and other tubers which they got from [the maguey] plant, all were kept in one part of the market in the place assigned to them . . . Let us go on and speak of those who sold beans and sage and other vegetables and herbs . . . and let us also mention the fruiterers, and the women who sold cooked food, dough and tripe in their own part of the market . . .*

Diego Rivera, the famous Mexican muralist, imagined how the bustling market at Tlatelolco might have appeared.

Traders at the markets also sold flowers and items for personal decoration, such as cochineal. Cochineal is a red to purple coloured dye made from the scale insect, which is a parasite that lives on cactuses. Aztec women dyed their teeth with cochineal to make themselves more attractive – a kind of lipstick inside the mouth. Many other dyes were sold at the markets, along with bark paper for writing. The vivid hues these dyes produced can be seen in the Aztecs' codices.

The Tlatelolco market was held every five days, and thousands attended, bartering, eating and drinking, and socialising. Tenochtitlán also had a large market, and smaller daily markets were dotted throughout the two cities. The Tlatelolco market was divided into areas for particular products. Finery made of gold and silver and other precious materials could be found in one part. Different kinds of meat – such as waterfowl, gophers, and dog – could be found in another. There were also whole separate markets dedicated to a district's specialty – for example, pottery, tools, or building materials.

Cotton was imported from lower lying areas outside the Valley of Mexico. The Aztecs didn't know about this material until they conquered the lands where it grew. Spinners turned the raw material into thread to be woven into cloth. Weavers incorporated brightly coloured feathers and dyed rabbit fur to make beautiful designs – such as seashells, whirlpools, butterflies, and geometric patterns – on cloaks and tunics.

MULTIPLE USES FOR MAGUEY

The spikey maguey plant grows to a great size, with its leaves reaching up to 2 metres in length. Rain in the Valley of Mexico is unreliable, but the maguey is drought-resistant. It can survive extreme cold and even hail, and grows in poor soils. The Aztecs used every part of it.

Women scraped the large maguey leaves to extract fibre, which they spun to create thread. They wove this on simple looms. Commoners used the resulting cloth to make clothes.

The maguey plant produces sap to feed its single, impressive flower, which blooms at the end of its life. Growers collected the sap – called *aguamiel*, which means 'honey water' – from the heart of the mature plant. They cut the plant at the base then scooped out the central stalk. Sap would then collect in the hole, producing up to 8 litres of *aguamiel* a day for four to six months.

Maguey sap could be reduced to syrup, an ingredient used in cooking. The plain, clear, fresh sap alone is very sweet, and is said to taste like the milk from a young coconut.

Maguey was also the central ingredient in *octli*, a popular alcoholic beverage similar to beer. White and frothy, it had a sour smell. It was sold in the eateries and bars that dotted the Aztec markets. To make *octli*, the sap from the plant was stored in pottery jars. After a day, it began to naturally ferment, creating the beverage. *Octli* had an alcohol content of 8–20 percent – strong stuff! This was fine for everyday consumption, but professional *octli* makers also produced the drink for rituals and festivals.

The hardy, drought-resistant maguey plant is still cultivated in Mexico. Though *octli* is seldom seen in Mexico today, certain varieties of maguey are grown to make the spirits mescal and tequila.

Aztecs made *octli*, an alcoholic beverage brewed from the sap of the maguey plant. It would have been served from jugs like this one.

Although drinking *octli* appears to have been widespread, and played a part in rituals and festivals, the penalty for public drunkenness was severe. Drunkards were thought to bring ruin to their families. A first offence for a commoner might see their head shaved – a public humiliation – or, if they were unlucky, their house demolished. A second offence was punished with death. The nobility was expected to set an example for others. Nobles who were drunk in public could expect to have their first offence punished with execution.

The technique of distillation – a method of separating alcohol out from other liquids – was introduced by the Spanish. Maize, honey, and cactus fruits provided the base for other fermented alcoholic drinks. Today, certain varieties of maguey are used to distil the spirits mescal and tequila.

This is Patecatl, god of the root of *octli*. There were so many *octli* gods, the Aztecs referred to them as *centzon totochtin* (400 rabbits). Patecatl's half-moon nose ring is typical of *octli* gods.

The Codex Mendoza shows an elderly woman drinking *octli*, an alcoholic beverage. Drunkenness was more tolerated in the elderly.

The four prone youths have been beaten to death as a punishment – some for theft, others for public drunkenness.

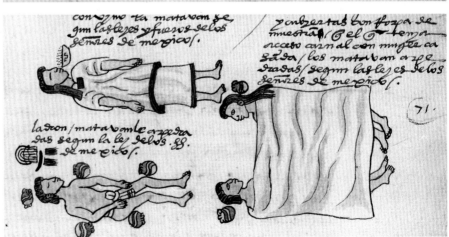

AMAZING MAIZE

Maize was by far the biggest crop in the Aztec Empire, as it still is in Mexico today. It was grown in several varieties in many colours – white, black, yellow, and red. Women ground maize to make that well-known Mexican food – the tortilla. They flavoured tortillas with another famous product of Mexico – chilli peppers. The Aztecs grew an enormous variety of these spicy, aromatic fruits. They combined them with tomatoes, avocados, cilantro, and other herbs to make salsas and other tasty fillings and sauces.

Women used clay cooking pots to make dishes like maize porridge. For *tamales* – a kind of dumpling – they made a maize dough and stuffed it with ingredients such as chillies, beans, squash, honey, or meats. It was then wrapped in a leaf and steamed or boiled.

Women had to spent a long time grinding maize kernels into flour and meal. To feed her immediate family, an Aztec woman would spend many hours every day just grinding. She would first need to boil the maize in water with mineral lime, then leave it overnight before bringing it to her grinding stone. This softened the maize so that the husks would come off easily. It also added calcium and released vitamin B12 (niacin) from the corn.

The resulting flour might be made into a maize gruel, flavoured with chillies, tomatoes, maguey syrup, and salt. Tortillas and beans formed another popular meal. Travellers took baked maize meal with them, mixing it with water to make an instant meal.

Aztec people mainly ate vegetables and grains, but many other foods – fish, waterfowl and their eggs, shellfish, crustaceans, turtles, frogs, quail, rabbits, and gophers – could be found in the markets. Although the Aztecs cultivated a huge variety of plants, they only domesticated two animals – turkeys and dogs. These could also be found for sale at markets, to be butchered later for meat.

Salt was another important ingredient in cooking. The Aztecs extracted it from the salty waters of Lake Texcoco. First they leached the water through a mixture of soils, resulting in a concentrated salty liquid. They then boiled and dried this to make crystallised salt.

At the time the Spanish conquistadors invaded, the Valley of Mexico fed well over a million people. The large number of people in the capital stimulated intensive farming in the surrounding area. And, of course, tributes drew in produce from outlying areas. The population had been growing dramatically for some time, and it must have seemed to the Aztec people that their empire could only continue to grow. Who was strong enough to challenge these mighty priests and warriors?

This carving of a locust shows the respect the Aztecs had for these creatures. Plagues of locusts are able to destroy crops, which must have been an impressive and fearful sight.

Only nobility and the wealthy owned exquisitely decorated ceramics like these. Highly skilled artisans, who could themselves become wealthy, lived in districts with a collection of workshops. These districts acted like European guilds, associations that looked after the interests of their members.

BITTER WATER

Cocoa is another food famously associated with the Aztecs. They usually drank it unsweetened, and their name for the drink translates as 'bitter water'. The Soconusco region, one of the outlying Aztec areas on the Pacific coast, grew the majority of cacao beans. Long-distance merchants traded in this prized food.

Only the nobility could afford to indulge in cocoa's exotic flavour. To make the drink, they first roasted the beans, ground them, then added cold water to the powder. Only occasionally did they sweeten it. Usually, they added chillies to heighten the taste. Another popular combination was to mix maize flour with cocoa powder to make a sort of thin gruel.

Cacao beans — the seeds from the large cacao pod — also acted as currency. The Spanish colonists recorded the value of exchange for these beans. A porter, the most common Aztec occupation, could expect to earn 100 cacao beans a day. This would buy a turkey hen or a hare. A large tomato cost one bean. Three beans bought a turkey egg.

The Aztecs enjoyed their cocoa frothy, by pouring the drink from a height.

51

A CROWDED COSMOS

The Aztecs had amazingly complex myths and religious practices, which they made even more elaborate by adopting gods from other peoples. Many Aztec gods had been worshipped for hundreds and sometimes thousands of years. The worship of Tláloc (god of rain and lightning), for example, dates back to the third century and the Teotihuacán civilisation.

Aztec gods were intense. Their passionate natures can be seen in Aztec stories around creation. There is more than one creation myth, and many variations. In the main story of creation, two founding deities emerged from the void – Ometecuhtli (lord of duality) and Omecíhuatl (lady of duality). Ometéotl (god of duality, literally 'two god') is the name used to represent both the male and female attributes.

Duality is commonly expressed throughout Aztec culture. This vessel shows a healthy living face on one side, and a dead and decomposing face on the other.

Quetzalcóatl, like many gods, could take various forms. One was Ehécatl (god of wind), who in one creation myth set the heavens in motion by blowing on them.

Examples of duality can be found throughout Aztec thinking and religious belief. They believed that balance between opposites helped to create order. Similarly, gods could be both creators and destroyers. Tláloc brought rains to make crops grow. But he could also devastate with floods.

Ometéotl had four sons, two of which – Quetzalcóatl (god of wind and wisdom), and Tezcatlipoca (god of war and destiny) – created further life. They made the first ancestors of people and the male and female gods of the underworld, Mictlantecuhtli and Mictecacíhuatl. Next Quetzalcóatl and Tezcatlipoca devised the calendar and created the sky and waters.

A huge crocodile-like creature with ferocious jaws at every joint, Tlaltecuhtli, floated on the Earth's waters eating everything the gods created. The four sons of Ometéotl killed her and her body became the Earth's surface.

THE FIVE
AGES

Next the four sons of Ometéotl created the five ages of the universe, known as the five suns. During each age, a different Aztec god served as the physical sun in the sky. The first four ages were cataclysmically destroyed, a result of in-fighting and jealousy between the gods.

The first age is Nahui Ocelotl (the Jaguar Sun), during which Tezcatlipoca (god of war and destiny) served as the sun. To become a sun, Tezcatlipoca had to agree to be sacrificed. He did this because after his death he would be reborn as the sun god. This idea of death followed by renewal was behind many Aztec rituals.

Tezcatlipoca only became half a sun when reborn – a rather inadequate addition to the sky. The gods then created the first humans for the world, who were huge in stature. These giants lived on acorns. Quetzalcóatl (god of wind and wisdom) became jealous of Tezcatlipoca and knocked him from the sky. Furious, Tezcatlipoca retaliated by sending jaguars to eat the giants and destroy the world.

During Toxcatl, a festival dedicated to Tezcatlipoca, a youthful captive warrior had the privilege of living the life of a god for a month before being sacrificed. He married four women, who represented four female deities. Magnificently attired on his last day, he passed through the streets in a procession, playing a flute. People bowed before him and ate dirt to show respect. He would then ascend the steps of the temple. At the top, the priests cut out his heart.

In the second age, Nahui Ehecatl (the Wind Sun), Quetzalcóatl served as the sun. He again created people, who this time were of normal size. They lived by eating piñon nuts. The people of this age became dishonest and immoral, so Tezcatlipoca turned them into monkeys. An enraged Quetzalcóatl sent hurricanes to destroy the monkeys and the world.

The third age bears the name Nahui Quiahuitl (the Rain Sun). This time, the god who became the sun was Tláloc (god of rain and lightning). The people he created ate aquatic plants to survive. In this age, Tezcatlipoca caused trouble again, stealing Tláloc's wife. A grieving Tláloc shone as the sun but wouldn't send any rain to Earth. Drought gripped the land. The people were transformed into dogs, butterflies, and turkeys. Tláloc's grief turned into rage and he destroyed the world with a great, fiery rain.

The fourth age is called Nahui Atl (the Water Sun), when Chalchiuhtlicue (goddess of rivers and lakes) became the sun. But Tezcatlipoca and Quetzalcóatl were jealous and tore her from the sky. They ripped a great hole in the sky, which let in a deluge, destroying the world and turning people into fishes.

The fifth age is Nahui Olin (the Earthquake Sun). This sun represents the present age, which the Aztecs believed would be destroyed by massive earthquakes. Self-important Tezcatlipoca offered himself again as the sun for this age. Other gods, however, preferred the humble god Nana-uatzin, whose name means 'full of sores'.

Here Mictlantecuhtli (god of death and lord of the underworld) stands grinning, with claw-like hands. Half his flesh has been ripped off, and his liver hangs out of his chest cavity. The Aztecs believed the liver contained a being's spirit. Mictlantecuhtli's grin may suggest a desire to torment. On one occassion he harassed Quetzalcóatl (god of wind, wisdom, and Venus) on his journey to the underworld. The holes in his head would have held curly black hair. Scientists have investigated residues on the statue, and found them to be human blood – during rituals the statue probably would have been doused in blood.

The gods built an enormous bonfire, so a god could be sacrificed to become the sun. Tezcatlipoca was meant to throw himself onto this fire, but at the last moment was gripped by fear. Nanauatzin proved the more courageous by jumping on the fire instead. Tezcatlipoca was struck with jealousy and also jumped in after him.

So two suns appeared in the sky, but two suns gave out too much light. The gods threw a rabbit into the face of Tezcatlipoca, dimming his light and turning him into the moon. He was now doomed to follow his brilliant fellow god across the sky.

After this, Quetzalcóatl (god of wind and wisdom) descended into the underworld to fetch some bones so he could create humans. But on his way out, Mictlantecuhtli (god of death) tormented and harassed him. Quetzalcóatl dropped the bones, shattering them into many different sizes – the reason why humans are different sizes.

Cihuacóatl (goddess of fertility and motherhood) then ground up the bones, and Quetzalcóatl pierced himself to mix in his blood. From this concoction they created humans.

SACRIFICING FOR LIFE

In the fifth age, Nanauatzin was now the only sun, and too weak to travel across the sky. The other gods sacrificed themselves, nourishing Nanauatzin with their blood. Filled with energy, he was then able to traverse the heavens.

This last part of the myth is crucial to understanding why sacrifice was so important to the Aztecs. The gods created humans then sacrificed themselves so that the sun could defeat the dark each day and bring life to the world. The Aztecs believed that as the gods went about their duties they became tired. Consequently, humans were needed to feed the gods with the life-essence of blood and nutritious hearts to replenish their strength, so that existence would continue. This, in turn, explained why the gods had created humans.

The Aztecs considered warfare itself to be sacred. They went into battle not just for conquest but also to capture prisoners to feed the gods. Warriors slain in battle were sacred because they had given their lives for the continuation of existence and were believed to rise with the sun god each morning to do battle with the darkness – mirroring what they had done on Earth. The deceased warriors did this for four years, after which they would be reborn on Earth as hummingbirds and butterflies.

The Aztecs didn't entirely trust their gods. They worried the world could end at any time because of the gods' continuous struggle against each other for control of the universe. If one succeeded over the others, the imbalance of power would result in a cataclysm. It's helpful to look at the Aztecs' religious behaviour in this context – they were constantly trying to appease impulsive gods, to nourish and strengthen an enfeebled sun, to balance an uncertain universe, and to control unstable elements.

The Aztecs also had a powerful belief in destiny and cosmic cycles. But it would be wrong to think that the Aztecs left everything up to fate. Even though they served the gods and sought to appease them with sacrifices, they also requested their help and guidance and tried to influence them. Gods and humans were interdependent.

MANY AND
MULTI-FACETED

Aztec gods can get confusing at times! They could take on different appearances depending on which of their characteristics they were expressing. And many of the gods had overlapping roles and powers.

All aspects of Aztec life had a religious element. Every occupation had a patron god. Cities, towns, and districts all had their respective gods. The gods could inhabit people, animals, inanimate objects, and the elements. Gods made the rain fall, crops grow, and the sun travel across the sky. Gods flooded rivers, and created wind and snow. They could be capricious, jealous, angry, adulterous, generous, grieving, cruel, kind, and nurturing. They were never indifferent.

The gods were involved in everything, which is possibly why the Aztecs had such a large number of deities. One Spanish chronicler counted the existence of over 2,000 gods in the geographic area that the Aztecs and neighbouring ethnic groups occupied. This is a staggering figure. Over the page you can read about the main gods the Aztecs worshipped and the various 'faces' each one could wear.

Scholars once thought this statue represented an elite eagle warrior. They now believe that it has even greater significance and is actually a representation of the sun god. The sun is the great warrior who rises in the east to slay the darkness and then flies across the sky, generating life and warmth.

Ometéotl

Tezcatlipoca

Quetzalcóatl

Xiuhtecuhtli

THE MAIN GODS

OMETÉOTL was the god of duality and the supreme deity. Ometecuhtli (lord of duality) was Ometéotl's masculine side; Omecíhuatl (lady of duality) the feminine side. Ometéotl was the ruler of the universe and had four sons.

TEZCATLIPOCA was the first born of Ometéotl. Tezcatlipoca means 'smoking mirror'. His name refers to obsidian — the black, volcanic glass the Aztecs used in weapons and as mirrors. Tezcatlipoca created the first humans and maize. He was also a god of war, destiny, and the planet Venus. He could take the shape of a jaguar.

QUETZALCÓATL, meaning 'feathered serpent', was the second son of Ometéotl. He was god of wind, wisdom, and, like Tezcatlipoca, a god of the planet Venus. Quetzalcóatl had been widely worshipped for hundreds of years before the rise of the Aztecs. Serpents feature prominently in Aztec myths as symbols of rebirth (think of a snake shedding its skin). Quetzalcóatl also created a earlier version of humans, and made the cosmos and the calendar. As Ehécatl, he was the god of the wind.

XIUHTECUHTLI was the god of fire and time. His name translates as 'lord of turquoise'. He also had a female aspect, Chantico, the goddess of the hearth. One of his most important guises was as Huehuetéotl, the old god of fire, who played a central part in rituals at the close of the Aztecs' 52-year calendar cycle. The Aztecs invoked Huehuetéotl each time they lit the fire at the ceremony to usher in the next cycle.

GODS THAT BRING LIFE

CHALCHIUHTLICUE, meaning 'wearer of the jade skirt', was Tláloc's wife. She was the goddess of rivers and lakes and gave protection to mothers during childbirth.

CINTÉOTL means 'god of maize'. As the staple crop of the Aztecs, maize was essential to life.

XOCHIPILLI, 'the flower prince', was the god of flowers, nobles, and music.

HUEHUECÓYOTL, meaning the 'old coyote', was also a god of music, though he was more crude than Xochipilli.

OMETOCHTLI, meaning 'two-rabbit', was the patron god of the 400 deities associated with the alcohol *octli*.

MAYAHUEL, Ometochtli's wife, was the goddess of the agave plant.

TETEOINNAN, meaning 'mother of the gods', had many forms. She was the protector of midwives and healing.

TLÁLOC was an ancient god and widely worshipped. His name means 'god full of earth'. He was the god of rain and lightning.

TLAZOLTÉOTL, meaning 'goddess of waste or filth', was the goddess of physical pleasure. She could forgive the crime of adultery – punishable by death.

COATLICUE, meaning 'goddess with the serpent skirt', was the mother of gods and a goddess of fertility. She gave birth to the moon, stars, and Huitzilopochtli (god of war). Even though she was a creator, she was also the destroyer of all things. Both the fertile womb and the devouring grave existed in her at once.

ITZPAPÁLOTL, meaning 'obsidian butterfly', was the goddess of ancestors and the Chichimecs (variously translated as 'barbarians' and 'nomads').

XOCHIQUÉTZAL, meaning 'quetzal-flower', was a mother goddess and a patroness of weavers and of prostitutes.

Tláloc

Huitzilopochtli

GODS REQUIRING SACRIFICES TO REPLENISH LIFE

TONATIUH, meaning 'sun', was the original sun of the fifth age in the Aztec myth of the world. He fed on blood and hearts so he could move across the sky.

HUITZILOPOCHTLI, meaning 'hummingbird of the left', was the god of war, and the Aztecs' principal god. In the later years of the Aztec Empire, he became associated with the sun.

MIXCÓATL, meaning 'cloud-serpent', was the god of ancestors and new beginnings.

TLAHUIZCALPANTECUHTLI, 'lord of the dawn', was the god of the planet Venus.

XIPE TÓTEC, 'our flayed lord', was a fertility god and a god of spring and renewal. He was also the patron god of combat.

MICTLANTECUHTLI, meaning 'lord of Mictlan', was the god of death and lord of the underworld. Mictlan was the lowest level of the underworld. Those who made it there would find eternal rest.

MICTECACÍHUATL, meaning 'lady of Mictlan', was the goddess of death and lady of the underworld.

TLALTECUHTLI, meaning 'lord or lady of the earth' was an earth god. Like other Aztec gods, Tlaltecuhtli had both a male and female aspect.

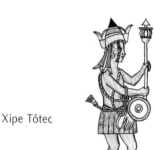

Xipe Tótec

Mictlantecuhtli

Coatlicue (the mother of gods, a goddess of fertility) conceived Huitzilopochtli (god of war).

DEFEATING THE DARKNESS

Huitzilopochtli, the god of war and the Aztecs' principal god, was the central player in another myth to explain the sun's passage across the sky. In the myth, Coatlicue (the mother of gods and a goddess of fertility) became pregnant while praying at a shrine on top of Coatépec (snake mountain). A ball of feathers floated down to her, which she put beneath her tunic. But when she went to retrieve the ball, it was gone and she had conceived a child. Her daughter, Coyolxauhqui (the moon), and sons (the stars), were ashamed of how she conceived the child and set out to murder her.

As Coyolxauhqui and her brothers tried to murder their mother, Huitzilopochtli leaped fully armed from her womb. He chopped his sister to pieces and her body parts rolled down to the bottom of the mountain. He then scattered the stars. Huitzilopochtli now dominated the sky, shining as the sun.

The Aztecs believed that the drama of the birth of Huitzilopochtli and his battle with his moon sister and star brothers was repeated each day at sunrise. The myth also determined the conduct of sacrifices to Huitzilopochtli on the Huey Teocalli. The side of the temple dedicated to Huitzilopochtli was conceived of as Coatépec (snake mountain). The victim was stretched over a stone at the top of the temple in front of the sanctuary of the god. His chest was sliced open and his heart offered to the sun. The priests then rolled the body down the temple, to the symbolic base of snake mountain. There it was received by a carved representation of the dismembered Coyolxauhqui. At the top of the temple, priests burned the heart, and the smoke rose to the heavens to sustain Huitzilopochtli as the sun god.

Some scholars have looked at the myth of Huitzilopochtli's birth in terms of gender. Women wield the forces of chaos and darkness. Men, on the other hand, defeat these forces and bring light and order into the world.

The Aztecs called women who had died in childbirth 'warrior women'. They believed these women accompanied the sun in the afternoon as it descended to be once again devoured by the darkness. These same women could become *cihuateteo* – demons that stole children and stalked crossroads at night to possess adults.

A *cihuateteo* is the demon spirit of a woman who had died in childbirth. Sculptures of *cihuateteo* could be found at intersections to ward off these evil spirits.

Coyolxauhqui is the moon goddess, and sister of Huitzilopochtli. This carved stone disc depicts her dismembered body after he chopped her to pieces. It would have sat at the base of the steps of the Huey Teocalli (Great Temple) ready to receive headless, sacrificial bodies. The symbolism represents Huitzilopochtli defeating the moon, an object of night, so that he could shine unopposed as the sun in the sky.

HEAVENS AND UNDERWORLDS

The Aztecs envisioned the Earth as an island surrounded by water. The heavens that rose above have been generally represented as containing 13 levels, although some versions have fewer. From their position at the zenith of the heavens, the duality gods – Ometecuhutli (lord of duality) and Omecíhuatl (lady of duality) – would send new spirits to be born on Earth.

The underworlds are usually depicted as having nine levels. The spirits of the dead had to endure a series of trials before they reached the last level and eternal rest with Mictlan-tecuhtli (god of death).

When you died, you could either go to the heavens or the underworlds. Where you ended up depended on how you'd died, rather than the life you had lived. For example, if you died by disease or accident, you were destined for the underworlds. If, on the other hand, you died in battle or childbirth you were elevated to the heavens to accompany the sun across the sky.

HEAVENS	UNDERWORLDS

Duality gods

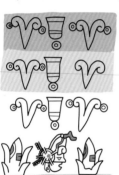

Red dwelling place

Yellow dwelling place

White dwelling place

Storms

Blue heaven of day

Green heaven of night

Comets

Venus

Sun

Stars

Moon

Earth and water

River

Mountains

Obsidian mountain

Slicing wind

Raised banners

Piercing arrows

Heart-devouring beast

Narrow passage

Mictlan (Eternal rest)

Some of the main elements of the Aztec cosmos. The Earth can be represented as a level of both the heavens and the underworlds.

AZTEC CALENDARS

The Aztecs had a system of two interlocking calendars. The first calendar was called the *xiuhpohuali*. It consisted of 18 months, each of 20 days, plus five extra days that didn't fit into the months, making up the 365 days of the solar year. Aztecs thought these extra five days held extremely bad luck. People fasted and avoided any activity on these days.

The *xiuhpohuali* dictated the main festivals and sacrifices. It determined when crops would be planted, when sacrifices were made to ensure plentiful rains, and the all-important rituals around the sun. Each of its 20 months was governed by one of the Aztec gods and had its own festival.

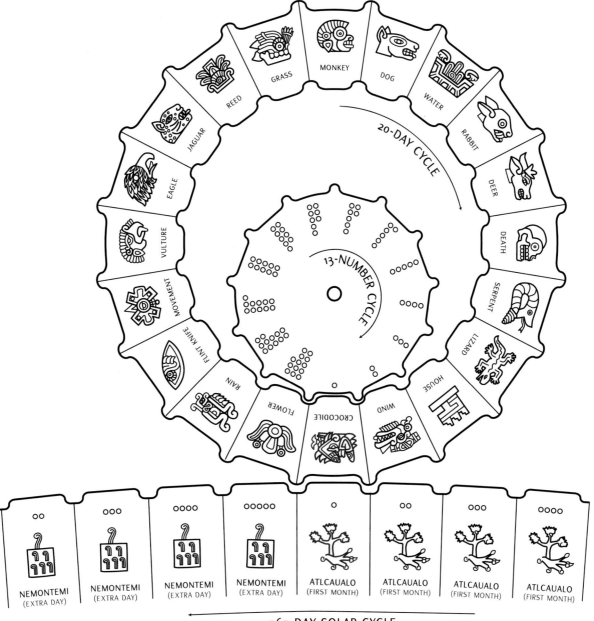

GRASS — MONKEY — DOG — WATER — RABBIT — DEER — DEATH — SERPENT — LIZARD — HOUSE — WIND — CROCODILE — FLOWER — RAIN — FLINT KNIFE — MOVEMENT — VULTURE — EAGLE — JAGUAR — REED

20-DAY CYCLE

13-NUMBER CYCLE

NEMONTEMI (EXTRA DAY) — NEMONTEMI (EXTRA DAY) — NEMONTEMI (EXTRA DAY) — NEMONTEMI (EXTRA DAY) — ATLCAUALO (FIRST MONTH) — ATLCAUALO (FIRST MONTH) — ATLCAUALO (FIRST MONTH) — ATLCAUALO (FIRST MONTH)

365-DAY SOLAR CYCLE

The second calendar, *tonalpohualli* (day count), was a sacred calendar. It was constructed from 20 signs and 13 numbers. Every sign and every number was associated with a different god, both of which influenced each birth date. On top of this, each 13-day week was governed by another god, giving 260 god combinations. When a child was born, the sign and associated number of their birthday were believed to determine their character, abilities, and destiny.

Every 52 years, the solar calendar and the sacred calendar aligned. This was a time of fear and uncertainty for the Aztecs. They extinguished their fires and broke all their pottery, believing the fifth sun – the present age – could potentially come to an end.

To ensure another 52 years of life, the Aztecs conducted the New Fire Ceremony. Priests waited for the constellation Pleiades to rise in the sky. They would then light a fire on the chest of a sacrificial victim, after which they cut out his heart and offered it to Huehuetéotl, the 'old god of fire'.

When the sun rose after the last night of the 52-year cycle, it confirmed the ritual's success and meant another 52 years of existence. People lit their fires again, from the sacrificial fire, and bought new pottery. It must have been a great relief.

The 52-year year calendar cycle was known as *xiuhmolpilli*, literally 'a bundle of reeds', which this carving depicts.

Aztecs raised some dogs specifically for food, but others were highly valued as companions. When a dog's master died, the dog would be sacrificed and cremated in a special ceremony, so it could guide its deceased owner through the perilous journey in the underworld.

Xiuhtecuhtli is the god of fire and time and protector of Aztec *huey tlatoque* (great leaders) and long-distance merchants. Like most of the gods, he could be helpful or harmful. As a fire in a hearth, he helped keep people warm and cook food. But he could also be an inferno that laid waste to homes.

This is Huehuetéotl, the old god of fire. During the New Fire Ceremony, he held the fate of humanity in his hands. The Aztecs adopted him as an aspect of Xiuhtecuhtli from the people who originally lived in Cuicuilco.

PLAYING BALL

The Aztecs played a fast and violent sport called *tlachtli*, which loosely translates as 'the ball game'. It was for both recreation and ritual. It has been suggested that the movement of the ball represented the sun, and the game was a re-enactment of the myth of Huitzilopochtli killing his sister after his birth – the victory of light over darkness. Sometimes the games were large public events that climaxed in sacrifice. Several forms of the game had been played for hundreds of years prior to the Aztecs' version. The Aztecs had two ball courts among their temples in the sacred centre of Tenochtitlán, which shows how important it was.

Two teams of players faced each other and knocked a solid rubber ball between them with their hips. They may have also used their elbows, knees, and head – but not their hands. The object of the game seems to have been to keep the ball in play.

The game was fast and violent. Players were protected by a large leather belt, but Spanish chroniclers in Mexico wrote that ball game players had enormous and constant bruises – some so large they had to be lanced. Players could even die as a result of the game.

Games between top teams had crowds watching on terraces above the brightly painted courts. Top ball game players became celebrities. Spectators vigorously gambled with one another, with some even betting themselves or their children. A codex of tributes records that 16,000 rubber balls were sent to Tenochtitlán in just six months.

Cortés took ball game players to Spain in 1528 as a spectacle for his monarch to enjoy. The speed and bounciness of the ball fascinated European viewers.

Centuries before the Aztecs, the Mayans added a stone ring to their own ball court (below). The Aztecs used two stone rings on some of their courts. A player knocking the ball through a ring brought instant victory for his team, but this was not the main objective of the game.

Xochipilli, god of games (above).

Codex Borbonicus shows the Aztecs' ball court (below).

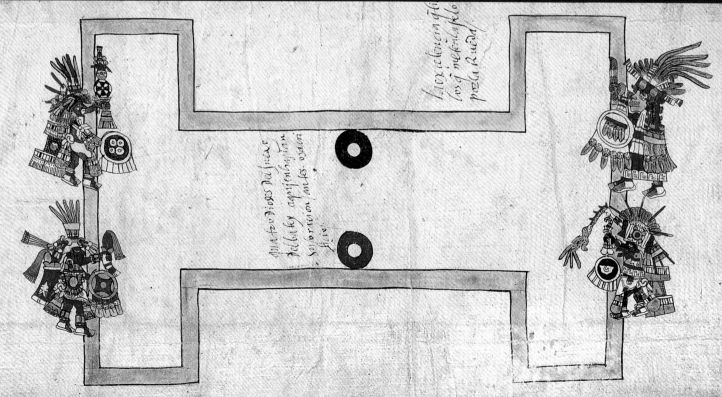

THE SCALE OF SACRIFICE

Human sacrifice had a deep religious significance in Aztec culture, and large public festivals with human sacrifice were common events. Exactly how much the Aztecs practised sacrifice has been hotly debated. Excavations between 1979 and 2007 of the Huey Teocalli (Great Temple) dedicated to Huitzilopochtli (god of war) and Tláloc (god of rain and lightning), found the remains of 126 sacrifices. The many other gods also required sacrifices at their smaller temples.

Some histories record that, in 1487, over 80,000 people met their end, sacrificed as a dedication to an extension of the Huey Teocalli. But such a large number of sacrifices for a single event is very doubtful. The sacred area around the Huey Teocalli could contain only a few thousand people at most. The entire region that the Aztecs ruled at the height of empire had a population of perhaps six million. Conducting large-scale sacrifices would have soon exhausted the pool of available victims.

So how did these rumours of thousands of victims at one time start? The conquering Spaniards might have exaggerated the 'mass slaughter' of innocent people to justify replacing the Aztec religion with their own. The different ethnicities in the surrounding city states may also have been keen to lay the blame for the introduction of sacrificial practices on the Aztecs, and that way avoid the scrutiny of the new, powerful conquerors.

Priests burned incense during ritual ceremonies. The atmosphere must have been intoxicating, with costumes and decoration, incense, music, dancing, and death.

WHO WAS SACRIFICED?

Aztecs sacrificed people from within their immediate community of Tenochtitlán as well as captives from other city states and tribes. The age, gender, physical qualities, and status of the person were all important in determining who was sacrificed at which festival.

A middle-aged Tenochtitlán woman of noble birth was chosen each year for sacrifice to ensure agricultural success.

Parents offered children if they met the criteria of having two cowlicks in their hair and had been born under a favourable sign. Their sacrifice to Tláloc (god of rain and lightning) was important because it guaranteed plentiful rains during the wet season. The clear, innocent tears the children shed during the ritual symbolised this rain. If they didn't cry on the way to being sacrificed, they might have their fingernails torn out as a prompt.

The Aztecs particularly valued albinos for sacrifice. Because the white skin of an albino indicated that they contained light, offering them strengthened the sun during frightening solar eclipses.

After the death of a king, the king's servants would be sacrificed so that they could help the monarch in the afterlife.

Priests took the lives of warriors captured during war to ensure the sun would rise – in other words, to make certain life would continue.

This pictogram shows a slave sacrificed at the funeral of his master. His heart has been removed from his chest and is spilling blood over his master's shrouded body.

Here a child is being sacrificed to Tláloc (god of rain and lightning).

69

As the Aztecs expanded their empire, they gained access to fresh supplies of sacrificial victims. By snatching people for sacrifices they made many enemies, particularly the Tlaxcalans. No one knows whether captured enemies willingly accepted their sacrificial fate. Some formed bonds with their captors, and, like the Aztecs, they probably would have viewed resistance as weak and dishonourable.

Interestingly, many Aztec people – musicians, prostitutes, priests – offered themselves willingly for death beneath the sacrificial knife. Sacrifice was not considered death but movement into another life. To be sacrificed, the Aztecs believed, made you divine. You rose to dwell within the levels of the heavens. The Aztecs likened this to a snake shedding its skin – shaking off an old life and becoming 'reborn'.

In addition, while on Earth, a sacrificial victim received special treatment up until their death – they were attended by priests, fed special foods, ritually bathed, and magnificently dressed. During the build-up to the sacrifice, participants might be involved in a dramatic enactment of mythical events. The Aztec people were constantly exposed to this sumptuous theatre. And the rituals around a volunteer's suddenly heightened, privileged life – and death – took place in the service of society at large and humankind in general. Once they had committed themselves to sacrifice, a person had a short future, but it would be intensely lived and coloured with supreme importance and passion.

METHODS OF SACRIFICE

The methods of sacrifice were as varied as the kinds of people chosen for this death.

The most common method of sacrifice involved cutting open the chest and removing the heart. But the Aztecs also practised other methods. They slit victims' throats, stretched and burned them over a bonfire, shot them with arrows, decapitated them, drowned them, compelled them to fight in ritualistic battles, starved them, and suffocated them. Sometimes a blazing fire would be kindled in a brazier, to incinerate hearts. The smoke would then rise into the sky, nourishing the gods. And it's likely they employed methods used elsewhere in the region, such as strangulation, disembowelment, and subjecting victims to steam.

Being sacrificed made you divine. This is why, at some festivals, people ate sacrificial victims — so they could join with the divine.

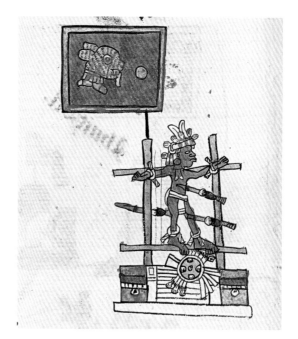

Removal of the victim's heart (top left) was the most common method of sacrifice.

A sacrificial victim (top right) is being shot with arrows before his heart is cut out. Another (bottom right) is being stretched over a fire before undergoing the same procedure.

A captured warrior has been given fake weapons (bottom left) to defend himself in a ritual battle. The jaguar warrior is about to 'scratch' him with a *macuahuitl*. At the conclusion of this battle, the captured warrior will be sacrificed by removal of his heart.

Tláloc (god of rain and lightning) shared equal place on the Huey Teocalli (Great Temple) with Huitzilopochtli (god of war), which shows how important he was to the Aztecs. Tláloc is typically represented with two fangs protruding from his mouth. Sacrificing children to him was especially important.

This reclining *chacmool* (sacrificial stone) has the face of Tláloc (god of rain and lightning) carved on it. On his abdomen is an elaborately decorated eagle vessel, which would have held the blood and hearts of those who had been sacrificed.

This is a *temalácatl* stone, which represented the sun. Captive warriors were tied to the stone to undergo ritual battle then sacrifice. During the mock battle, an Aztec warrior 'scratched' the captive and his blood spilled onto the stone and nourished the sun.

Xipe Tótec (god of spring and renewal) took a central place in a ceremony of great significance for the Aztecs — Tlacaxipehualiztli (flaying of men). In keeping with another of Xipe Tótec's roles as the patron god of combat, the sacrificial victims first had to be defeated in a ritual battle. Priests then sacrificed the victims by removing their hearts, before skinning their bodies. The priests wore the skins of the victims' faces over their own faces and draped the skins of the bodies over their shoulders. They wore these for the full 20 days of the month. At the conclusion of the festival, they emerged reborn from the rotting skin. From death comes life. The ritual was likened to a corn husk being removed so its seeds could germinate, or a snake shedding its old, dead skin to emerge 'renewed'.

The conquest of Tenochtitlán (right).

This mask made out of a human skull and pierced with the blades of sacrificial knives is thought to represent Mictlantecuhtli (god of death). It had been placed as an offering in the Huey Teocalli (Great Temple).

Aztecs used flint knives to slice open the chest of sacrificial victims and remove the heart. Flint is a very hard form of quartz. Special flint blades inlaid with a face like these, however, were used as offerings in the Huey Teocalli (Great Temple).

CONTACT AND CONQUEST

In the ten years prior to the Spanish arrival, Aztec priests had seen several ill-fated omens: a comet blazing in the sky, lightning strikes burning down temples, water surging up from Lake Texcoco to flood houses, and a pillar of flame that appeared on the horizon at night but disappeared in daylight. At night time in the Aztec capital, a wailing woman was heard to cry, 'Oh my children, where will I take you?' Strange stories of floating mountains and towers in the sea inhabited by bearded men had reached Tenochtitlán and Moctezuma II, the *huey tlatoani*. It is even said that hunters caught a grey crane on Lake Texcoco that had a mirror in its head. They took it to Moctezuma II who looked into the mirror and saw visions of a great war.

The Florentine Codex showing a comet blaze in the sky — an omen of sickness, famine, and war.

A prophecy foretelling the return of Quetzalcóatl (god of wind and wisdom) in 1519 and the influence it had on Moctezuma II's reaction to the Spanish conquistadors who marched into Tenochtitlán that same year has been the subject of debate. Did he really think Hernán Cortés was the god Quetzalcóatl returning to claim the throne as legend had foretold? Did he greet him as a god and pledge loyalty to him? A number of historians have questioned whether this was the case. Perhaps the Aztecs used the prophecy to explain events after the fact, as a way of understanding how the fierce and intelligent Moctezuma II could have been blindsided by the clever Spaniard.

Moctezuma II was an educated man, a sophisticated leader, and an experienced military campaigner. Is it possible he simply didn't know how to respond to a violent and effective force in his empire? The stories of the powerful cannons and giant 'deer' on which the Spanish rode may have affected him. He had dealt with many other kings and warlords from a wide variety of ethnicities. It's reasonable to assume that he had a clear-headed understanding of potential threats and invaders. Cortés was another man of war, but unlike anything Moctezuma II had ever experienced.

The fall of Tenochtitlán and the demise of the Aztec Empire took just two years. Despite the speed and ferocity of the Spanish conquest, the outcome wasn't a foregone conclusion when the conquistadors first landed on the Mexican coast. Cortés overcame considerable obstacles to bring down the Aztec Empire –

and he had astonishingly good luck along the way. He wasn't an experienced military commander, although he seems to have had a natural ability in this field. His small force was vastly outnumbered in combat. He had to traverse large distances of unfamiliar and difficult country, with most of his soldiers on foot and wearing armour. And he escaped annihilation by a whisker on many occasions.

On Cortés's side were superior armaments – cannons, steel swords, steel armour, and warhorses – and an extreme discontent among many of the local tribes who the Aztecs had conquered. They were impoverished by tributes and stung by their people – especially their children – being taken for sacrifice.

Cortés's personality was another critical factor in the conquistadors' success. He had a cool head in battle and the ability to respond quickly to changing circumstances. His bold leadership and strategic diplomacy with the Aztecs' enemies also played a part in the fall of the once great empire. As did disease – smallpox, introduced by the Spanish, ravaged the indigenous population, killing perhaps a quarter of the people in the Valley of Mexico.

MISSION VERSUS AMBITION

Governor Velázquez of the Spanish colony in Cuba – and Hernán Cortés's brother-in-law – commissioned Cortés's expedition to the Mexican coast. The purpose was to establish trading relations with the tribes that lived there. But it appears that Velázquez became suspicious of Cortés's motives. Whoever seized the mainland of the Americas for Spain could expect glory and fantastic wealth. Velázquez may have wanted this honour for himself. He tried to revoke the commission, but Cortés resisted, sailing for Mexico on 18 February 1519.

Cortés had 11 ships in his fleet, with a complement of 100 sailors, some 550 soldiers, which included 30 crossbowmen and 12 arquebusiers (the arquebus is an early kind of firearm), and as many as seven cannons. A doctor, carpenters, at least eight women – who appear to have been either nurses or fighters – some 300 Cubans and a handful of African slaves and freemen completed the company. Another crucial piece of this fighting unit was a contingent of warhorses.

Hernán Cortés, leader of the Spanish invasion.

THE POWER
OF WORDS

En route, Cortés spent some time on Cozumel, an island in the Caribbean Sea, attempting to convert the locals to Christianity. While there, he heard about a couple of Spanish shipwreck survivors living in Yucatán on the mainland and sent messengers to negotiate their release. One of the survivors, Gerónimo de Aguilar, returned with the messengers. In his years with a local tribe he had learned to speak the Mayan language, and of course he also spoke Spanish. One of the key pieces for Cortés's success had just fallen into place.

From Cozumel, Cortés sailed around the Yucatán Peninsula, landing at Potonchán. There he fought and defeated a local Mayan tribe in two battles. By way of reconciliation, they gave him a gift of slaves, who included a woman named Malinalli. Nahuatl (the Aztec language) speakers called her Malintzin, and she was later called La Malinche in Spanish.

This is the second vital piece that would aid Cortés's success, for although La Malinche couldn't speak Spanish, she could speak both Mayan and a Nahuatl dialect. Now Cortés could communicate with Nahuatl speakers, first talking to Aguilar, who translated into Mayan for La Malinche to translate into Nahuatl. The arrangement may have been awkward, but it worked.

La Malinche eventually learned Spanish. She must have been a sharp and perceptive person. As well as translating, she advised Cortés on local customs and how the indigenous people thought about and viewed the world. This was crucial intelligence. She may also have saved his life in Aztec-controlled Cholula. Cortés was often referred to as 'Malinche' by the locals.

La Malinche gives us the origin of a Mexican word: a 'malinchista' is defined as a traitor. Its more general meaning is someone who mimics the language and customs of another people. Mexican feminists and other contemporary thinkers have attempted to rehabilitate La Malinche's reputation. After all, many tribes wished to rebel against the despotic Aztec rule and she assisted with this. The thousands of indigenous male warriors and the kings who also supported Cortés are not subject to the same condemnation. In many respects, La Malinche was the most powerful woman in the Valley of Mexico at the time.

With Aguilar and La Malinche, Cortés marched to Cempoala, a city state of the Nahuatl-speaking Totonac people. City dignitaries and cheering crowds greeted Cortés. Here he learned of the powerful Aztec Empire. The Aztecs had subdued the Totonacs, raiding their territory several times in the preceding decades to capture victims for sacrifice. The Totonacs were particularly incensed by the seizure of their children.

Cortés's encounter with the Totonacs was also the beginning of the clash of religions that characterised the meeting of Spanish and indigenous cultures. Cortés forbade sacrifice, and his soldiers pushed the stone idols from the top of the Totonac temple, erecting a cross in its place.

This 1926 painting of Cortés and La Malinche is by the Mexican painter Jose Clemente Orozco. La Malinche was, of course, more than a translator – she was also Cortés's counsellor, cultural adviser, and mistress. The prone figure at their feet may symbolise the overwhelmed people of Mexico. The couple represent the beginning of the *mestizos* in Mexico, people of mixed ethnic and cultural descent.

The Totonacs were outraged at the destruction of their idols. But Cortés won them over, explaining that they would be brothers under his god and promising that he would oppose Moctezuma II. He may have sealed their trust when he daringly arrested and imprisoned Aztec tax collectors who had come to collect taxes from the Totonacs. To provide insurance against retaliation from Moctezuma II, he later, secretly, let two of them go. The Totonacs eagerly allied with the fearless Spanish against the Aztecs.

Cortés also enlisted their help to build a settlement, Villa Rica de la Vera Cruz (Rich Town of the True Cross), where he constituted a municipal council. The council then elected him as an *adelantado*, a military title allowing him to become governor of land he conquered. With this title Cortés could effectively sidestep any restrictions that Velázquez had placed on his commission.

At this time, ambassadors from Moctezuma II were sent to greet him. The two parties exchanged gifts – including hammered gold discs the size of table tops. Cortés attempted to impress them with a display of firepower from his cannons, aiming them into the jungle and smashing down trees. He also had his small cavalry gallop up and down the beach. The ambassadors were dumbfounded. Their artists quickly painted these scenes and they were given to runners to present to Moctezuma II. Later, more ambassadors arrived, with more lavish gifts and even more gold.

There is no doubt the golden gifts would have alerted Cortés to the riches that awaited him in the Aztec capital. Moctezuma II probably intended the gifts to show his might. But Cortés seems to have interpreted the gesture as a sign of fear and weakness.

Also around this time, Cortés got into the first serious trouble with his men. Those loyal to Velázquez planned to take a ship and return to Cuba. Cortés ruthlessly quashed the mutiny by hanging two of the conspirators, flogging two others, and mutilating the feet of another. He then made an astounding move – he scuttled all but one of his ships! Any return to Cuba was impossible – the success of the expedition became vital. Failure could mean death.

He loaded the remaining ship with a portion of gold he owed to the Spanish Crown, and this sailed for Spain. He left a hundred men at Villa Rica de la Vera Cruz, and, with an escort of Totonac guides and warriors, began the long march to Tenochtitlán.

Codex Duran shows the arrival of the Spanish at Yucatán Peninsula in present-day Southeast Mexico.

Workshops of Aztec goldsmiths turned out finely crafted jewellery like this pendant in the shape of a shield and this bracelet. The gifts that Moctezuma II sent to Cortés included large gold discs and at least 20 figurines of animals made out of gold.

THE HATED AZTECS

From the Totonacs, Cortés had learned that the confederation of tribes from Tlaxcala had a special hatred for the Aztecs. For years the Tlaxcalans had been subject to 'flower wars' with the Aztecs. The purpose of these pre-arranged battles was not victory, but the capturing of warriors for sacrifice. Because of the sacred status of warriors, they were the most valuable sacrificial victims.

The Aztecs had vanquished the city states around Tlaxcala, surrounding them with an economic blockade. The Tlaxcalans believed it was only a matter of time before they too fell to their mighty enemy, and some historians have wondered why they hadn't already. Some speculate that the Tlaxcalans were too strong; others suggest that the Aztecs wanted to keep the confederation intact so the flower wars would continue providing them with a fresh supply of captured warriors. Whatever the reason, the Tlaxcalans had been impoverished by the Aztecs and resented them deeply.

Cortés would have to pass through the Tlaxcalan territory on his way to Tenoch-titlán. When he entered their land, he met a hostile force comprised of tens of thousands of Tlaxcalan warriors. Despite the vast numbers of the enemy, Cortés managed to hold them at bay. Many days of fierce battles followed, during which Cortés led his men on a retributive raid on Tlaxcalan villages, burning them and killing civilians.

A faction within the Tlaxcalan forces proposed they withdraw and ally themselves with these skilful soldiers. The Tlaxcalans retreated. When the Spanish entered Tlaxcala, the rulers welcomed them as heroes.

After resting and regrouping, Cortés marched to Aztec-controlled Cholula, his force strengthened by Tlaxcalan warriors. He received a frosty reception when they entered the city. The Cholulan leaders offered the Spanish neither food nor drink. La Malinche relayed a rumour to Cortés that the locals intended murdering the conquistadors while they slept. An angry Cortés confronted the city's leaders and accused them of treachery. His soldiers then killed several of the nobles and set the city alight. In a letter to the Spanish king, Cortés claimed that, with the help of the Tlaxcalans, he went on to kill 3,000 warriors in the city.

He then sent a message to Moctezuma II that he had been disrespected in Cholula. He went on to say that if the Aztecs treated him with respect and gifts of gold, they need not fear the punishment he had meted out in Cholula. It became obvious to Moctezuma II that the many gifts of gold he'd already sent Cortés were not going to dissuade him from marching on Tenochtitlán. He seemed to have no option but to invite the conquistador to the capital.

CORTÉS'S ARRIVAL

Cortés, his soldiers, and several thousand Tlaxcalan warriors arrived at Tenochtitlán on 8 November 1519. The city was an astonishing sight to the Spanish. They looked upon the immense size of the place, the exactness of the architecture, the orderly layout of houses and canals, and the industrious population with amazement. Moctezuma II took Cortés 'by the hand' and gave him and his soldiers a tour of the city.

Moctezuma II hosted Cortés, his soldiers, and the Tlaxcalan warriors at his father's palace. The conquistador engaged Moctezuma II and his council in several days of talks. He demanded more gold, which he received. Then, on 14 November, Cortés again struck with a bold move. He took Moctezuma II hostage. He imprisoned the Aztec *huey tlatoani* in the palace he was using as a barracks, and then demanded a stack of gold, which was handed over. Cortés now effectively oversaw Tenochtitlán through Moctezuma II.

This situation lasted for eight months, until April 1520 when Cortés received word that Pánfilo de Naváez, a Spanish commander, had arrived on the Mexican coast. He had with him a force of 900 soldiers and orders to arrest Cortés for treason. Velázquez had made his move on his brother-in-law. Naváez had also brought smallpox with him.

Cortés's response was yet another daring act of decisiveness. Leaving 140 men and some Tlaxcalan warriors under the command of his friend Pedro de Alvarado, he marched from Tenochtitlán to face Naváez on the coast. This is an arduous trek over mountain ranges reaching several thousand metres in elevation. The speed with which he executed this manoeuvre is probably what gave him

an advantage. With a small force of some 260 men, he surprised Naváez in a night attack. Cortés defeated Naváez, imprisoning him in Villa Rica de la Vera Cruz.

Along with his other abilities, Cortés must have had a powerful gift for persuasion – some might say manipulation. He convinced the defeated commanders of Naváez's force to join him. In return, he promised them incomparable wealth – the gold of Tenochtitlán.

He marched with this expanded force over the mountain range once more and back to Tenochtitlán. On arriving in the capital, Cortés encountered rebellion. In his absence, Alvarado had massacred much of the leading nobility while they celebrated a festival in the temple of Huitzilopochtli (god of war).

The Aztecs claim that Alvarado led an unprovoked attack, greedy for the gold and jewels the worshippers wore. Alvarado justified his actions to Cortés as a pre-emptive strike to quell a planned rebellion. A lot of doubt has been cast on Alvarado's version of events. Alvarado, his men, and the Tlaxcalans were now besieged in their palatial accommodation. Although Moctezuma II had managed to broker a truce, intermittent fighting continued.

Moctezuma II received Cortés in person.

MOCTEZUMA'S DEATH

Debate, mystery, and myth surround how Moctezuma II died. In Cortés's account, he persuaded the great Aztec leader to speak to the people gathered before the palace. He wanted Moctezuma II to convince them to allow the conquistadors to leave for the coast in peace. When he stepped onto a balcony, Moctezuma II was met by a hail of stones hurled by the crowd. Badly injured, the *huey tlatoani* refused treatment and, during the days after this event, willed himself to die.

Desiring death would have been in keeping with Moctezuma II's religious beliefs. He may have hoped to roam in the cornfields of the heavenly plane of Cincalco, as had the Toltec king Huemac. This fate was reserved for the victims of certain sacrifices, and possibly suicides. Scholars have found striking parallels between the Toltec king's heroic suicide and the Aztecs' later account of Moctezuma II's death.

Some accounts, made well after the event, claim that the conquistadors speared and killed the *huey tlatoani* before fleeing the palace. Cortés had certainly proved unscrupulous when it served his purpose. Perhaps Moctezuma II's usefulness had run out. Perhaps the show of public scorn confirmed to Cortés that the *huey tlatoani* no longer held any sway with his people.

Or was there a more sinister intention in killing him? Perhaps Cortés wanted to deny the *huey tlatoani* his 'passive suicide' as a final humiliation. No one knows for certain what happened to Moctezuma II's body afterwards.

NIGHT OF SORROWS

With water and food dwindling in the besieged palace and the Aztecs' patience obviously at an end, Cortés chose to escape. On 1 July 1520, during a rain storm, the Spanish snuck out of the palace. They proceeded down the road over the lake that led to the nearby city Tlacopan. The Aztecs soon realised Cortés had escaped and pursued him.

The Aztecs rained arrows on the conquistadors from canoes on the lake. The Spanish infantry, left behind by Cortés and others on horseback, hacked their way through the hordes of warriors. Many infantrymen, weighed down by armour and gold, drowned – the Aztecs had removed bridges on the roads to prevent their flight. Some historians speculate, given the sheer numbers killed,

The Battle of Otumba, which followed Cortés's bloody retreat from Tenochtitlán, could have spelled his end. However, the Aztecs withdrew, allowing the exhausted and wounded conquistadors to escape to Tlaxcalan territory.

that the gaps may have been bridged by corpses, aiding some to escape. As many as 600 Spanish died and over 1,000 Tlaxcalans. It can be assumed that as many Aztecs also lost their lives. The Spanish dubbed the event *La Noche Triste* (The Night of Sorrows).

The fighting continued on the mainland. The Tlaxcalans led the Spanish on a route that would take them to safe ground. The Aztecs pursued and a huge battle ensued on the plain in Otumba. In the open ground, the armoured warhorses and their armour-clad riders with their iron-bladed lances and swords came into their own. Cortés led charge after charge, smashing and cutting his way through the masses of Aztec warriors.

But even warhorses could be overcome by Aztec warriors. One of Cortés's soldiers described warriors wielding their 'broad-swords' against a cavalryman:

> *Pedro de Morón was a very good horseman, and as he charged with three other horsemen into the ranks of the enemy the Indians seized hold of his lance and he was not able to drag it away, and others gave him cuts with their broad-swords, and wounded him badly, and then they slashed at the mare, and cut her head off at the neck so that it hung by the skin, and she fell dead.*

The majority of the Aztec army was comprised of commoners, who served in the military in times of war and as part of their tribute to the state. The elite warrior orders, however, were composed of professionals, some of whom were military commanders. The most elite were the jaguar warriors, the eagle warriors, and, leading them all, the *cuahchicqueh* (the shaved ones). The *cuahchicqueh* had shaved heads with only a braid of hair over their left ear. The top

These eagle and jaguar warriors are each brandishing a *macuahuitl*, a lethal hardwood weapon edged with razor-sharp obsidian.

generals came from this order. They painted their heads blue on one side and red or yellow on the other. They vowed, under pain of death from their fellow warriors, that they would never step backwards in battle.

Eventually, in the Battle of Otumba, the Spanish recognised an Aztec general among the fighters. They killed him, and the Aztecs withdrew. The Spanish escaped to the lands of the Tlaxcalans.

Nearly everyone who had escaped the Battle of Otumba had been wounded. While his armies recovered, Cortés plotted with the Tlaxcalan leaders to crush the Aztecs. The Tlaxcalans generally agreed that the Aztecs would be out to get revenge and eventually engage them in total war. They backed Cortés.

One thing puzzled Cortés during his period of recovery in Tlaxcala: why hadn't the Aztecs continued their attack? It was both out of character for these fighting people and tactically unwise. With the Spaniards severely weakened from their escape from Tenochtitlán it would have been the prime moment to strike.

Cortés didn't know that the Aztecs were fighting another enemy: smallpox. It's thought that an African slave from Naváez's expedition, killed when Cortés and his men escaped from the Aztec capital, was sick with the disease. The Aztecs probably became infected when they looted his body. The capital was reeling from this new foe.

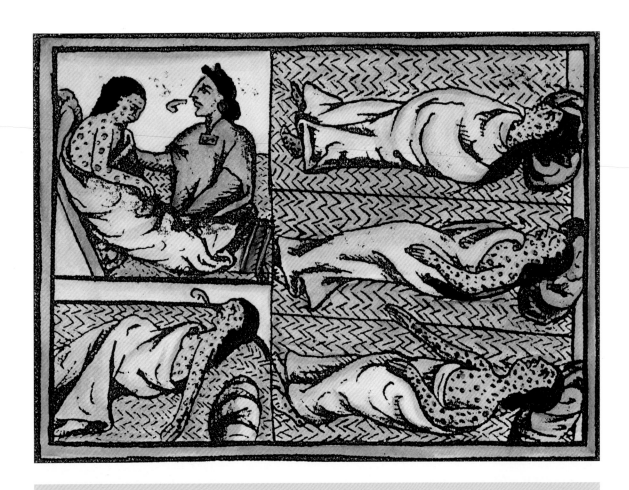

The Spanish text accompanying this image from the Florentine Codex reads, 'The Great Dying'. The smallpox epidemic laid waste to the indigenous population. It has been estimated that it killed a quarter of the people in Mexico. The sufferers are smothered in the large 'blisters' the disease produces.

This steel armour breastplate belonged to Pedro de Alvarado, the most prominent figure in the Spanish invasion after Cortés. The Aztecs called him Tonatiuh (sun) because of his blond hair.

This is a *chamfron*, an armoured headpiece for a horse. When the Aztecs first saw horses, they thought the Spanish rode on the backs of huge deer. The fully armoured cavalrymen and horses initially aroused awe and fear in the Aztecs — they eventually overcame their fear, and attacked cavalry and infantry with equal fury.

THE SIEGE OF TENOCHTITLÁN

In a military tactic familiar to the Aztecs, Cortés began knocking over outlying states to encircle and isolate Tenochtitlán. He sent one of his commanders with Spanish soldiers to liberate Chalco from their Aztec overlords. Chalco became their ally and other small tributary states followed such as Tepeyac, Yauhtepec, and Cuauhnahuac. And with each Spanish victory, the Aztecs were weakened, unable to call on warriors from states they used to dominate. Eventually only Tenochtitlán and its sister city Tlatelolco remained.

Cortés now devised a plan to attack the cities that stood at the end of the roads that crossed Lake Texcoco. He would then control the land routes into Tenochtitlán. The first battle was to take Tlacopan, which supplied water to Tenochtitlán.

The Spanish lost the initial battle, but Cortés adjusted his strategy and pressed on. After a great many battles, the Spanish held Tlacopan and all the cities at the main roads leading to the capital. They broke the aqueduct that supplied water. Only canoes could now bring supplies to Tenochtitlán, and the Tlaxcalans strangled this lifeline with their own canoes.

As he had done before, Cortés introduced a surprising and brilliant element. Prior to the siege, he had ordered his master shipbuilder to build 13 brigantines – small ships that can be powered by oars and sail – in Tlaxcala and had transported them to the capital

in pieces. They were armed with cannons. But even then the Aztecs found ways of stifling them. They plunged pointed sticks into the lake and, when a brigantine became stuck, they would attack and overwhelm the vessel.

Towards the end of the grinding 80-day siege, conditions within the city were abysmal. People died of starvation. There was no clean drinking water. Entire families died of smallpox. There were so many bodies that often people weren't buried. Their houses were simply demolished over them.

To make matters worse for the warriors, the Aztec leadership was thin. Alvarado's massacre in the temple of Huitzilopochtli had taken out many key people. Smallpox further weakened the chain of command. It killed Huey Tlatoani Cuitlauac – Moctezuma II's successor.

On several occasions, Cortés sent envoys to try to negotiate surrender, but the Aztecs refused. This wasn't a compassionate gesture on Cortés's part. The city represented a great prize, one that he could boast about to his monarch. It would be a great pity to destroy this wonder.

The city eventually fell on 13 August 1521. Cuauhtemoc, cousin of Moctezuma II and the last *huey tlatoani*, surrendered. The Tlaxcalans had little sympathy for their bitter enemies. They looted the city and showed no mercy to Aztec warriors. Perhaps 100,000 people died of starvation, war, and disease. The great city of Tenochtitlán lay in ruins. The Aztec Empire had fallen.

ECHOES OF
THE AZTECS

After the overthrow of the Aztec Empire, the conquering Spanish set about suppressing the Aztec religion. They broke idols and temples and used the rubble as foundations for churches and other buildings. Friars burned the codices, the books the Aztecs wrote using coloured illustrations and glyphs (pictograms and symbols). The missionaries replaced the old objects of worship with equivalents from their own religion – crucifixes, churches, and Bibles. They built their churches on the sites of the Aztec temples.

For some time, the Aztecs in urban areas simply practised their rituals in secret.

They also used other clever tactics, such as building figures of their gods into the walls of churches, and placing stone carvings of their gods face down as the bases for the pillars in these same buildings. Another ploy was to put religious codices inside crucifixes. So while they appeared to be worshiping the Christian god, they could at the same time worship their own deities.

A SYNTHESIS OF RELIGIONS

Eventually, the Aztec beliefs and practices began to change and blend with the introduced Catholic religion. Some of the old gods disappeared, such as Huitzilopochtli, god of war and the principal god of the Aztecs. Although it could be argued that he does have a contemporary presence in the imagery on the Mexican flag and coat of arms, representing his prophecy which found the Aztec homeland.

Unlike the urban areas, rural villages didn't suffer the same degree of suppression and destruction. Farmers and other inhabitants continued worshipping as they had in the past. Some of the old gods continue to this day. Often they exist in altered forms and have sometimes been blended with Christian symbols and concepts.

In northern Veracruz, descendants of the Aztecs worship a god they call Ometotiotsij ('honoured two-god'). Their practices make it clear that this is the original creation god Ometéotl (god of duality). A version of Chalchiuhtlicue (goddess of rivers and lakes) is worshiped throughout much of Mexico. The sun, of such immense significance to the Aztecs, still finds expression in ritual today. Some worshippers make a circular altar on top of a pole and place offerings on it. Streamers radiate from it like sunbeams. In Spanish, these Aztec descendants call their sun god 'Jesus'.

Blood rituals haven't entirely disappeared, either. Goat blood is sometimes spilled on altars in present-day Mexico to encourage crops to grow. The Aztecs are well known for human sacrifice, but they also performed animal sacrifices. Priests and others would also at times spill their own blood in ceremonies.

Spanish friars burned Aztec codices as part of an attempt to end Aztec religious practices, which they considered evil and gruesome. Ironically, they also made records of Aztec culture and religion in codex form, with accompanying commentary in Spanish. They sought to better understand Aztec religion so they could more effectively dismantle it. Yet it's their codices that have supplied much of what we know about Aztec belief and culture.

Atrium crosses, like this one, date from after the Spanish conquest, and would have been fashioned by indigenous carvers. No two are the same. They may feature depictions of flowers, vegetables, and Jesus, along with symbols of his death and resurrection. Atrium crosses take their name from their placement in the centre of an atrium that was part of a larger religious compound. The locals would gather to worship in the atrium while the church and other buildings were being completed.

Part of the Spanish strategy for spiritual conquest was to reuse sacred Aztec objects in Catholic rituals. Here, a sculpture of the feathered serpent god Quetzalcóatl (god of wind and wisdom) has been hollowed out and turned into a baptismal font.

The Virgin of Guadalupe, depicted with a blending of Catholic iconography and Aztec symbolism. She has dark skin and is radiating sunlight.

The Virgin of Guadalupe is a religious icon that is a synthesis of Aztec and Catholic symbolism. Accounts written a century after the event tell how the indigenous peasant Juan Diego saw a vision of the Virgin Mary on Tepeyac Hill in Mexico in 1531. Later, an image of the Virgin miraculously appeared on his cloak. Sceptics point to earlier accounts that identify it as a painting made by a local indigenous artist called Marcos.

In the 16th century, the icon drew crowds of indigenous converts to the church on Tepeyac Hill. It had been built on the site of a temple dedicated to Tonantzin (goddess of motherhood). Rather than Mary, the worshippers referred to the image as Tonantzin. Some worshippers also referred to the image as the Mother of Maguey. This icon is now displayed in the Basilica of Our Lady of Guadalupe. It attracts millions of pilgrims from around the world each year.

During the Mexican War of Independence (1810–21), the Virgin of Guadalupe adorned the flags of Mexican freedom fighters. She had become a unifying national symbol. In 1999, Pope John Paul II named Our Lady of

Guadalupe the patroness of the Americas. So this image with echoes of Aztec religious practice now takes a central place in Mexican Catholic worship.

The Day of the Dead celebration also melds Aztec and Spanish culture. During the days leading up to this ritual, people make altars dedicated to departed family and friends. These are elaborately decorated with skulls made of sugar and marigolds. Photographs of the dead are placed on the altars along with offerings of their favourite food and drink to entice their spirits to return to Earth. Even pillows and blankets may be laid out to provide a place for the weary spirits to rest after their long journey from the land of the dead.

The day coincides with the Catholic All Saints Day, which is followed by All Souls Day. All Saints Day celebrates those who have attained sainthood, and All Souls Day remembers those who have died. The Day of the Dead can be seen as a version of All Souls Day, but with a distinctively Mexican cultural sensibility.

One of the characters that symbolises the Day of the Dead is Catrina – an elegantly dressed skeleton. Her image appears in street murals and on plates and lollipops, women dress as her, and there are Catrina dolls. In Aztec mythology, Mictecacíhuatl (goddess of death) took care of the bones in the final level of the underworld. A significant Aztec festival was dedicated to her. Catrina can be seen as a popular expression of Mictecacíhuatl in a celebration that blends Aztec cultural expression with a Catholic holiday.

About 1.5 million Mexicans still speak Nahuatl, the Aztec language. This is a significant cultural heritage, and literally echoes the Aztec world. Nahuatl has entered the school curriculum, where it is spoken and taught alongside Spanish.

Catrina, the 'elegant skeleton', appears everywhere in Mexico during the Day of the Dead. Printmaker and cartoonist José Guadalupe Posada made the original zinc etching *La Calavera Garbancera* (above) on which Catrina is based around 1910, the beginning of the Mexican Revolution. He took a swipe at the rich who adopted European (therefore un-Mexican) dress and manners.

Although the word is seldom used in Mexico today, the concept of the *mestizo* is a way of further understanding the blending of cultures. During Spanish colonial rule, the colonists developed a caste system. Its basic outline had four levels. Those born in Spain were at the top. People with European parents born in New Spain (Mexico) were on the next rung. *Mestizos*, those of mixed Indian and Spanish blood, came next. And indigenous people were at the bottom, and had the least rights and respect.

By 1810, *mestizos* formed the majority of the population. After the Mexican War of Independence that dislodged Spanish rule, they became a dominant force. Successive governments tried to forge a national identity that interwove the various cultural strands that now existed in Mexico and were implied by this term. *Mestizo* came to mean a person of mixed descent and cultures rather than someone of mixed races. It facilitated both diversity and synthesis within the Mexican culture.

Many of the examples of cultural expression above show the pride Mexican people feel in their heritage. And in Mexico City today, they literally stand at what was the very centre of one of the greatest civilisations that has ever existed.

Modern Mexico City covers the area where Tenochtitlán once was.

TIMELINE:
THE AZTECS IN
WORLD HISTORY

12,000—5000 BCE
Nomadic hunter-gatherer peoples populate Mesoamerica.

10,000 BCE ▼

60,000—50,000 BCE
The earliest Aboriginals settle in Australia.

c 1000 CE
A nomadic group sets out from the mythical homeland of Aztlán, guided by their patron god, Huitzilopochtli. They call themselves the Mexica, but come to be known as Aztecs.

900—1200 CE
The Toltec culture dominates Mesoamerica, and they build the city of Tula.

1325 CE
The Aztecs settle on an island in Lake Texcoco. They begin to construct their capital city, Tenochtitlán, and the Huey Teocalli (Great Temple).

1428 CE
The Triple Alliance is formed between the cities of Tenochtitlán, Texcoco, and Tlacopan. The Aztec Empire begins to expand rapidly.

1452—54 CE
Famine follows prolonged drought and a severe flood in Tenochtitlán.

1000 CE ▼

AZTEC EMPIRE 1325—1521 CE

1206 CE
Genghis Khan becomes the ruler of the Mongol Empire.

c 1230—1282 CE
Ancestors of the Māori first arrive in New Zealand.

1300—1600 CE
The European Renaissance flourishes.

1430—1533 CE
The Inca become a dominant power in South America. The Spanish conquer the Incas in 1533.

1485—1603 CE
The House of Tudor rules England.

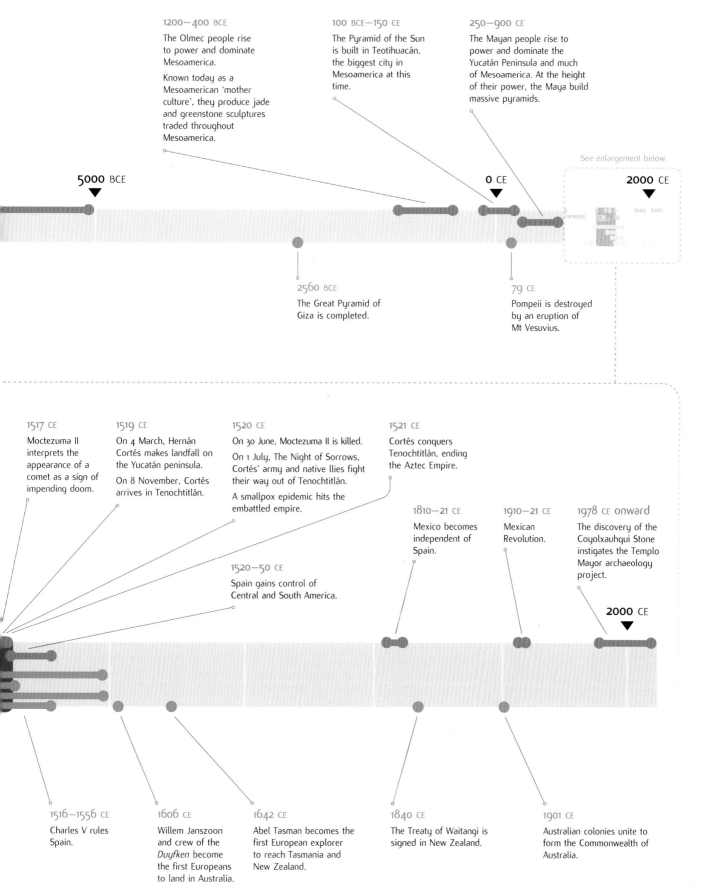

1200—400 BCE

The Olmec people rise to power and dominate Mesoamerica.

Known today as a Mesoamerican 'mother culture', they produce jade and greenstone sculptures traded throughout Mesoamerica.

100 BCE—**150** CE

The Pyramid of the Sun is built in Teotihuacán, the biggest city in Mesoamerica at this time.

250—900 CE

The Mayan people rise to power and dominate the Yucatán Peninsula and much of Mesoamerica. At the height of their power, the Maya build massive pyramids.

See enlargement below

5000 BCE

0 CE

2000 CE

2560 BCE

The Great Pyramid of Giza is completed.

79 CE

Pompeii is destroyed by an eruption of Mt Vesuvius.

1517 CE

Moctezuma II interprets the appearance of a comet as a sign of impending doom.

1519 CE

On 4 March, Hernán Cortés makes landfall on the Yucatán peninsula.

On 8 November, Cortés arrives in Tenochtitlán.

1520 CE

On 30 June, Moctezuma II is killed.

On 1 July, The Night of Sorrows, Cortés' army and native llies fight their way out of Tenochtitlán.

A smallpox epidemic hits the embattled empire.

1521 CE

Cortés conquers Tenochtitlán, ending the Aztec Empire.

1810—21 CE

Mexico becomes independent of Spain.

1910—21 CE

Mexican Revolution.

1978 CE onward

The discovery of the Coyolxauhqui Stone instigates the Templo Mayor archaeology project.

1520—50 CE

Spain gains control of Central and South America.

2000 CE

1516—1556 CE

Charles V rules Spain.

1606 CE

Willem Janszoon and crew of the *Duyfken* become the first Europeans to land in Australia.

1642 CE

Abel Tasman becomes the first European explorer to reach Tasmania and New Zealand.

1840 CE

The Treaty of Waitangi is signed in New Zealand.

1901 CE

Australian colonies unite to form the Commonwealth of Australia.

IMAGE AND OBJECT CREDITS

front cover
Sun stone, *c* 1500, Aztec, stone, Museo Nacional de Antropología, image Museum of New Zealand Te Papa Tongawera, photographer Jeff Fox

p 1
Eagle warrior, *c* 1440–69, Aztec, fired clay, stucco & pigment, 1700 x 1180 x 550mm, Museo del Templo Mayor 10-220366, INAH, photographer Michel Zabé

p 2
Xochipilli pectoral pendant, *c* 1200–1521, Mixtec, gold, 73 x 42 x 10mm, Museo de las Culturas de Oaxaca 10-105724, INAH, photographer Michel Zabé

p4
Mural of the Aztec market of Tlatelolco, 1945, Diego Rivera, Palacio Nacional, Mexico City © Banco de México, 'Fiduciario' en el Fideicomiso relativo a los Museos Diego Rivera y Frida Kahlo, Av. 5 de Mayo No. 2, Col, Centro, Del. Cuahtémoc 06059, México

p 7
Screen with scenes from the conquest of Mexico (detail), late 1600s–early 1700s, oil on canvas, Museo Nacional de Historia, Castillo de Chapultepec, Mexico City, INAH, photographer Jesús López

p 8
Consejo Nacional para la Cultura y las Artes, INAH

p 9
Codex Boturini, *c* 1530–1541, pen & ink on paper, Museo Nacional de Antropología, INAH, image The Art Archive, Alamy

p 10
Heart sculpture, *c* 1500,

Aztec, jade, 240 x 200 x 110mm, Museo Nacional de Antropología 10-392930, INAH, photographer Jorge Vértiz

p 11
The Granger Collection, New York

p 12
Handwritten manuscript, *c* 1862, Lady Elizabeth Phillips (transcriber), Jay I Kislak Collection, Library of Congress, Washington DC

p 13
Frank Burek, Corbis

Eagle *cuauhxicalli* (sacrificial vessel), *c* 1502–1520, Aztec, basalt, 82 x 139 x 76mm, Museo del Templo Mayor 10-252747, INAH, photographer Michel Zabé

p 14
Map © Museum of New Zealand Te Papa Tongarewa, illustrator Luke Kelly

p 15
Dennis MacDonald, Alamy

Mark D Callanan, Getty Images

p 16
Glyphs © Museum of New Zealand Te Papa Tongarewa, illustrators Fay & Walter

p 17
The John Montgomery Drawing Collection, Foundation for the Advancement of Mesoamerican Studies Inc. www.famsi.org

p 18
Codex Telleriano-Remensis, folio 31r, Bibliothèque Nationale de France, image Foundation for the Advancement of Mesoamerican Studies Inc. www.famsi.org

p 19
Codex Ixtlilxochitl, folio 106r, Bibliothèque Nationale de France

p 20
Codex Mendoza, *c* 1541–42, pen & ink on paper, DEA Picture Library, The Granger Collection, New York

p 21
Serpent warrior standard bearer, *c* 1500, Aztec, basalt, 525 x 290 x 190mm, Museo Arqueológico del Estado 'Dr Román Piña Chan' A-52207, INAH, photographer Michel Zabé

p 22
Codex Mendoza, *c* 1541–42, pen & ink on paper, DEA Picture Library, The Granger Collection, New York

p 23
Cactus sculpture, *c* 1500, Aztec, stone, 970 x 280mm, Museo Nacional de Antropología 10-220928, INAH, photographer Michel Zabé

p 24
Family tree of great rulers © Museum of New Zealand Te Papa Tongarewa, illustrators Fay & Walter

p 25
Warrior head with lip plug, *c* 1500, Aztec, fired clay, 195 x 153 x 188mm, Museo Nacional de Antropología 10-392909, INAH, photographer Michel Zabé

Lip plug with figure of a cox-cox bird, *c* 1200–1521, Mixtec, jade & gold, 43 x 11mm, Museo de las Culturas de Oaxaca 10-105540, INAH, photographer Michel Zabé

p 26 clockwise from top left

Ring with figure of a descending eagle, *c* 1325–1521, Mixtec, gold, Museo de las Culturas de Oaxaca 10-106165, INAH, photographer Michel Zabé

Ear ornaments, *c* 1500, Mixtec, gold, 13 x 39mm each, Museo de las Culturas de Oaxaca 10-105428 0/2, INAH, photographer Michel Zabé

As credited p 2

p 27
Codex Mendoza, *c* 1541–42, pen & ink on paper, Bodleian Library, Oxford

pp 28–29
Island Capital of the Aztecs, Tenochtitlan (mural), Luis Covarrubias, 1919-1987, Museo Nacional de Antropología, INAH, photographer Javier Hinojosa

p 30
Portrait of Moctezuma, late 1600s, Antonio Rodríguez, oil on canvas, Museo degli Argenti, Florence, image The Art Archive, Alamy

p 31
Codex Mendoza, *c* 1541–42, pen & ink on paper, Bodleian Library, Oxford

p 32
Codex Borbonicus, folio 23 (detail), pen & ink on paper, Bibliothèque de l'Assemblée Nationale, Paris

Xilonen ceremonial vessel, *c* 1500, Aztec, fired clay & pigment, 990 x 600 x 490mm, Museo Nacional de Antropología 10-583437, INAH, photographer Michel Zabé

p 33
Macehual (commoner) figure, *c* 1500, probably Aztec, stone, 470 x 199 x 130mm, Fundación Televisa 21 pj 31,

98

CONACULTA-INAH FOTOTECA CNME, photographer Gliserio Castañeda García

Macehual head, *c* 1500, probably Aztec, stone, 227 x 222 x 252mm, Fundación Televisa 21 pj 107, CONACULTA-INAH FOTOTECA CNME, photographer Gliserio Castañeda García

p 34
Florentine Codex, vol. 7, folio 16v, 1577, ink on paper, Biblioteca Medicea Laurenziana, Florence

p 35
Codex Mendoza, folio 58r, *c* 1541–42, pen & ink on paper, Bodleian Library, Oxford

Inge Johnsson, Alamy

p 36
Codex Mendoza, folio 58v, *c* 1541–42, pen & ink on paper, Bodleian Library, Oxford

p 37
Flute, *c* 1496–1520, Aztec, fired clay & pigment, 35 x 52 x 185mm, Museo del Templo Mayor 10-253047, INAH, photographer Jorge Vértiz

p 38
DEA Picture Library, De Agostini Picture Library, Getty Images

p 39
Partial cross-section of the Huey Teocalli (Great Temple), 1900s, French, Archives Larousse, Paris, Giraudon, image The Bridgeman Art Library

p 40
Offering, *c* 1325–1502, Aztec, 540 x 1260 x 1060 mm, Museo del Templo Mayor 10-252003, INAH, photographer Michel Zabé

Commemorative plaque, 1487, Aztec, diorite, 920 x 620 x 300mm, Museo Nacional de Antropología 10-220919, image Mary Evans, Iberfoto

p 41
The four zones © Museum of New Zealand Te Papa Tongarewa, illustrators Fay & Walter

p 42
The Art Archive, Alamy

p 43
Agricultural goddess sculpture, *c* 1500, Aztec, stone, 700 x 240 x 210mm, Fundación Cultural Televisa, 21 pj 4, CONACULTA-INAH FOTOTECA CNME, photographer Gliserio Castañeda García

The Granger Collection, New York

p 44
Anne Lewis, Alamy

Florentine Codex, vol. 3, folio 30v, 1577, ink on paper, Biblioteca Medicea Laurenziana, Florence, image Alamy

p 45
As credited p 4

p 46 clockwise from top left
LeighSmithImages, Alamy

Frans Lemmens, Alamy

Gina Martin, National Geographic Stock

Gina Martin, National Geographic Stock

p 47
Keith Dannemiller, Corbis

Jug, *c* 1500, fired clay and pigment, 375 x 355 x 325mm, Fundación Cultural Televisa 21 pj 105, CONACULTA-INAH FOTOTECA CNME, photographer Gliserio Castañeda García

p 48
Pulque deity sculpture, *c* 1469–81, Aztec, basalt & pigment, Museo del Templo Mayor 10-162940, INAH, photographer Michel Zabé

Codex Mendoza, *c* 1541–42, pen & ink on paper, Bodleian Library, Oxford

p 49
Locust sculpture, *c* 1250–1521, Aztec, stone, 327 x 281 x 505mm, Fomento Cultural Banamex AC PH 01-0293, INAH, photographer Michel Zabé

p 50
Vessel, *c* 1500, fired clay & pigment, 373 x 428mm,

Fundación Cultural Televisa 21 pj 10, INAH, photographer Michel Zabé

Vessel, *c* 1500, fired clay & pigment, 355 x 400mm, Fundación Cultural Televisa 21 pj 35, INAH, photographer Michel Zabé

p 51
Greg Elms, Loney Planet Images, Getty Images

Codex Tudela, folio 3r, 1553, vellum, Museo de America, Madrid, Spain, image The Bridgeman Art Library

p 52
Figure with three faces, *c* 1300 (contested), Aztec, fired clay & pigment, 180 x 220 x 90 mm, collection from Direccion de Artes Visuales UNAM 08-741814, image INAH, photographer Michel Zabé

p 53
Quetzalcóatl sculpture, *c* 1250–1521, Aztec, basalt, 700 x 490 x 440mm, Centro Regional Cultural Apaxco 1-10832, image The Art Archive, Alamy

Duality vessel, *c* 1250–1521, Matlatzinca, fired clay, 180 x 114 x 140mm, Museo Arqueológico del Estado 'Dr Román Piña Chan' A-52115, INAH, photographer Michel Zabé

p 54
Tezcatlipoca effigy pot, *c* 1500, Aztec, fired clay and pigment, 145 x 175 x 170mm, Fundación Cultural Televisa 21 pj 71, INAH, photographer Michel Zabé

p 55
Mictlantecuhtli sculpture, *c* 1480, Aztec, fired clay, stucco & pigment, 1760 x 800 x 500mm, Museo del Templo Mayor 10-264984, INAH, photographer Michel Zabé

p 57
As credited p 1

pp 58–59
The Art Archive, Alamy

Codex Magliabecchi, folio 76, image INAH

p 60
Coatlicue sculpture, *c* 1325–1521, stone, image The Art Archive, Alamy

p 61
Cihuateteo sculpture, *c* 1500, Aztec, stone, 1120 x 530 x 530mm, Museo Nacional de Antropología 10-97810, INAH, photographer Michel Zabé

Coyolxauhqui stone, *c* 1325–1521, Aztec, stone, 3200mm diameter, Museo del Templo Mayor, INAH, photographer Jorge Vértiz

p 62
Heavens & underworlds © Museum of New Zealand Te Papa Tongarewa, illustrators Fay & Walter

p 63
Tonalpohuali calendar © Museum of New Zealand Te Papa Tongarewa, illustrators Fay & Walter

p 64
Dog sculpture, *c* 1500, Aztec, stone, 475 x 200 x 290mm, Museo Regional de Puebla 10-203439, INAH, photographer Michel Zabé

Xiuhmolpilli (bundles of reeds), *c* 1500, Aztec, stone, 383 x 300 x 223 mm, Fundación Cultural Televisa 21 pj 9, CONACULTA-INAH FOTOTECA CNME, photographer Gliserio Castañeda García

p 65
Xiuhtecuhtli sculpture, *c* 1469–81, Aztec, basalt, 325 x 190 x 190mm, Museo del Templo Mayor 10-220357, INAH, photographer Michel Zabé

Huehueteotl sculpture, *c* 1486–1502, Aztec, basalt, Museo del Templo Mayor 10-212978, INAH, photographer Michel Zabé

p 66
Tuul, Robert Harding World Imagery, Corbis

Image Source, Corbis

p 67 clockwise from top left
Private Collection, Peter Newark American Pictures, The Bridgeman Art Library

The Bridgeman Art Library, Alamy

Codex Borbonicus, The Art Archive, Alamy

p 68
Censer, 1325–1521, Aztec, fired clay & pigment, 74 x 610 x 2270mm, Museo Nacional de Antropología 10-220158, INAH, photographer Michel Zabé

p 69
Primeros Memoriales, folio 250r, Fray Bernardiono de Shahag, Patrimonio Nacional

Codex Magliabecchi, folio 66, Biblioteca Nazionale Centrale di Firenze

p 70
Florentine Codex, vol. 1, folio 25r, 1577, ink on paper, Biblioteca Medicea Laurenziana, Florence

p 71 clockwise from top left
Codex Magliabecchi, XIII, II, 3, p 70, 1904, Library of Congress, Washington DC

Codex Telleriano-Remensis, folio 41v, Bibliotheque Nationale de France, image Foundation for the Advancement of Mesoamerican Studies Inc. www.famsi.org

Codex Duran, folio 280, *c* 1581, ink on paper, National Library of Spain, image INAH

Codex Duran, folio 53, *c* 1581, ink on paper, National Library of Spain

p 72
Tláloc pot, *c* 1440–69, Aztec, fired clay & pigment, 300 x 350 x 315mm, Museo del Templo Mayor 10-220302, INAH, photographer Michel Zabé

Chacmool, c 1500, Aztec, stone, 740 x 1080 x 450mm, Museo Nacional de Antropología 10-109410, CONACULTA-INAH FOTOTECA CNME, photographer Gliserio Castañeda García

p 73
Temalácatl, c 1250–1521, Mixtec, stone, 865mm, Museo de las Culturas de Oaxaca 10-105130, INAH, photographer Michel Zabé

Xipe Tótec sculpture, *c* 1250–1521, Aztec-Matlatzin, stone, 410 x 320 x 220mm, Museo Arqueológico del Estado de México 'Dr. Román Piña Chan' A-51956, INAH, photographer Michel Zabé

p 74
Skull mask, *c* 1250–1521, Aztec, human skull, silex, shell & pyrite, 190 x 127mm, Museo del Templo Mayor 10-162934, INAH, photographer Michel Zabé

Ceremonial knifeblades with faces, 1325–1521, Aztec, flint, obsidian & resin, INAH, image The Art Archive, Alamy

p 75
The Conquest of Tenochtitlan (detail), oil on panel, 1600s, Jay I Kislak Collection, Library of Congress, Washington DC

p 76
Florentine Codex, 1577, ink on paper, Biblioteca Medicea Laurenziana, Florence, image The Art Archive, Alamy

p 77
The Art Archive, Alamy

p 78
La Malinche & Cortes (fresco), 1926, Jose Clemente Orozco, SOMAAP, licensed by Viscopy, 2013, image Schalkwijk, Art Resource

p 80
Codex Duran, folio 197r, *c* 1581, ink on paper, Biblioteca Nacional, Madrid, image The Bridgeman Art Library

p 81
Pendant in the shape of a shield, *c* 1500, Aztec-Mixtec, gold, silver & copper, 105 x 85mm, Museo Baluarte de Santiago 10-213084, image The Bridgeman Art Library

Bracelet, *c* 1500, Aztec-Mixtec, gold, silver & copper, 48 x 70mm, Museo Baluarte de Santiago 12-213113, INAH, photographer Hector Ceja

p 83
The Meeting of Cortés and Moctezuma, c 1650–1700, Mexico, oil on canvas, Jay I Kislak Collection, Library of Congress, Washington DC

p 84
Classic Image, Alamy

p 85
Florentine Codex, 1577, ink on paper, Biblioteca Medicea Laurenziana, Florence, image The Art Archive, Alamy

p 86
Florentine Codex, 1577, ink on paper, Biblioteca Medicea Laurenziana, Florence, image The Granger Collection, New York

p 87
Armoured breastplate of Pedro de Alvarado, 1500s, Spanish, iron, 420 x 340mm, Museo Nacional de Historia, Castillo de Chapultepec 10-233988, INAH, photographer Jorge Vértiz

Chamfron (armoured headpiece) for a horse, early 1500s, Spanish, riveted & burnished wrought iron, 320 x 562 x 335mm, Museo Nacional de Historia, Castillo de Chapultepec 10-92271, INAH, photographer Jorge Vértiz

pp 88–89
Screen with scenes from the conquest of Mexico, late 1600s–early 1700s, oil on canvas, Museo Nacional de Historia, Castillo de Chapultepec, Mexico City, INAH, photographer Jesús López

p 90
Kenneth Garrett, National Geographic Stock

p 91
Codex Tlaxcala, folio

242r, 1500s, Diego Munoz Camargo, pen & ink on paper, Glasgow University Library, Scotland, image The Bridgeman Art Library

p 92
Atrium cross, *c* 1600, colonial, stone, 1560 x 910 x 360mm, Museo Regional de Tlaxcala 10-341001, INAH, photographer Michel Zabé

Baptismal font, *c* 1521, Mexica, volcanic stone, 350 x 1350mm, Museo Nacional del Virreinato 10-544945, INAH, photographer Jorge Vértiz

p 93
John Collier Jr, Corbis

Virgin of Guadalupe, *c* 1730s–80s, Nicolas Enriquez, oil on canvas, private collection, image Christie's Images, The Bridgeman Art Library

p 94
La Calavera Catrina, *c* 1910–13, Jose Guadalupe Posada, zinc etching, Private Collection, Giraudon, image The Bridgeman Art Library

Hemis, Alamy

p 95
dbimages, Alamy

pp 96–97
Timeline © Museum of New Zealand Te Papa Tongarewa, illustrated by Luke Kelly

back cover
As credited p 30

As credited pp 28–29

As credited p 55

EXHIBITION ACKNOWLEDGEMENTS

SECRETARÍA DE EDUCACIÓN PÚBLICA

Emilio Chuayffet Chemor
SECRETARIO

CONSEJO NACIONAL PARA LA CULTURA Y LAS ARTES

Rafael Tovar y de Teresa
PRESIDENTE

INSTITUTO NACIONAL DE ANTROPOLOGÍA E HISTORIA

María Teresa Franco y González Salas
DIRECTOR GENERAL

Cesar Moheno
SECRETARIO TÉCNICO

José Francisco Lujano Torres
SECRETARIA ADMINISTRATIVO

COORDINACIÓN NACIONAL DE MUSEOS Y EXPOSICIONES

Marco Barrera Bassols
COORDINADOR NACIONAL

Paola Albert
DIRECCIÓN DE EXPOSICIONES

Leticia Pérez Castellanos
SUBDIRECTORA DE EXPOSICIONES INTERNACIONLES

Erika Gómez Carbajal
COORDINADORA DEL PROYECTO

Raúl Barrera
CURADOR

INSTITUCIONES PARTICIPANTES INAH

Museo del Templo Mayor
Museo Nacional de Historia Castillo de Chapultepec
Museo Nacional de Antropología
Museo Nacional del Virreinato
Museo Regional de Puebla
Museo de las Culturas de Oaxaca
Museo Regional de Tlaxcala
Museo Regional Michoacano
Museo Regional de Guadalajara
Museo Regional de Chiapas
Museo Baluarte de Santiago – Veracruz
Museo Arqueológico de Tula
Museo de la Escultura Mexica 'Eusebio Dávalos'
Biblioteca Nacional de Antropología e Historia
Dirección de Salvamento Arqueológico
Zona Arqueológica de Teotihuacán

OTRAS INTITUCIONES PRESTATARIAS

Museo Arqueológico del Estado de México – 'Dr. Román Piña Chan'

Museo de Antropología del Estado de México

Centro Regional Cultural Apaxco

Fundación Televisa

Banco Nacional de México S.A. BANAMEX

Dirección General de Artes Visuales

INDEX

Page numbers in **bold** indicate illustrations.